NATHANIEL A. TURNER, J.D.

RAISING SUPAMAN

First Printing, 2014

ISBN 978-0-9895879-1-4

The Raising Supaman Project

11805 North Pennsylvania

Carmel, IN 46302

www.raisingsupaman.com

Cover design by Matt Vincent, themattvincent.wordpress.com

Edited by Alyson Cunningham,

Prepared for publication by Naeem Khari Turner-Bandele

Dedication

This book is dedicated to none-other than Naeem Khari Turner-Bandele, a.k.a *Supaman*, to whom I owe an extreme debt of gratitude. Thank you for being a cooperative and forgiving M.I.T. (Man in Training), while I attempted to figure out through trial and error how to best serve as your father, mentor and friend.

I love you now and I have loved every moment of your existence - from the day I learned of your conception to this very moment as we travel to Brazil where you will begin another exceptionally exciting chapter of your life. Your journey to Brazil, at this particular time, has left me as confident as I have ever been about your extraordinarily bright future, your progress as a true citizen of the world, and as the man I have always envisioned you becoming.

I am so proud of you that there are no words that I know of that can adequately express my feelings. I am equally grateful that God has allowed me to be your father. All I can say is that it has been and remains my distinct honor and privilege to raise you, Supaman.

Contents

Chapter 1: As a Man Thinketh

Naeem:

First, I want you to know that your apprehension when it came to running today, your fear of competition and your lack of poise in simply seizing the moment has no appreciable effect on my feelings about you. Rest assured, I will never allow anything to make me question the value and purpose of my relationship with you. Without question, my love for you is on par with the great loves any father could ever and has ever had for his son. So relax, I'm in this fight with you for the long term.

Instead, I will admit that I am perplexed by my inability to convey and instill in you the hope and belief that you possess the capacity to do far greater things than your fears and reservations currently allow you to imagine. At the moment, I realize that I must develop better parental tools if you are ever to maximize your ability. Your words and actions today are proof of my parental inadequacies and I must – I will - rectify them immediately.

I should have been more observant, as the signs of a tentative competitor were noticeable. I should have recognized the manifestations of lingering doubt and the presence of the fear and loathing growing inside you. I should have listened better as the way in which you spoke was a hint that you had unwarranted reservations. Although I heard you loud and clear, my expectation was that you would deliver your own self-motivated message.

I hoped and prayed that your training had equipped you to speak words of empowerment to yourself—words to remove all doubt and reservation—words that would encourage you to discontinue the conception and belief in negative thoughts. My hope was that at the very moment doubts began to creep in, you would have replaced those thoughts with positive affirming beliefs – ideas that breathe life not death, thoughts of having both feet in and beliefs of only success. Instead, it appears that my hopes were unrealized thus my inadequacy as your father and mentor are now obvious, and were on full display during the track meet. I am sorry for failing to recognize your fears and doubt. I am sorry for failing you. I will be better!

Internal Drive

Secondly, I want you to know that I heard you completely when you expressed your feelings about what you considered your internal drive. For the record—internal drive is not doing what you are instructed to do. Internal drive, when called into question, is not proved by defensive posturing: simply offering words without evidence of consistent and unrelenting deeds. Internal drive is not waiting for someone who will receive little or no benefit from your progress and success to do all the work to prepare you to succeed. Internal drive does not require fear from an outsider or worries of being punished.

Internal drive is doing what others won't do without having to be poked and prodded; emailed and texted; yelled at and punished. Internal drive is expressed and is evident by a non-stop, passionate, purposeful, focused, refusal to be outworked; an uncompromising unwillingness to give less than one's best; an un-matched pride in seeking all available options to be successful; and a goal driven desire to simply maximize one's potential and ability. Internal drive is at the very least sharing and taking a 50/50 or better role in your own success.

Internal drive is *"I will because I need to…"* Internal drive is *"I will because there is no choice for me other than to give all I can give"*. Internal drive is *"I will because quitting and more importantly the thoughts of quitting cannot and will never be tolerated"*. Internal drive is never thinking or saying the words, *"I will try"*. Rather internal drive maintains the thought *"I must, I will no matter what may come my way…by any means necessary"*. The aforementioned is what it means to have internal drive. So please don't tell me for one minute that you believe the words you spoke about internal drive were valid.

Obedience

Let me be absolutely clear, what you did today when you went to the track meet with your mother was simply obey authority; it was nothing more. There was nothing that you did that should be equated with internal drive.

Obedience will not and cannot ever be equated with internal drive. Rarely are we praised or awarded for obedience alone. Only in a society where expectations are unreasonably and unacceptably low do we find rewards for being obedient; doing what is expected—a minimal performance standard if you will.

As an example, at your school's most recent Honor's Convocation, I did not see any student rewarded for doing the minimum. An institution that prides itself on espousing that their minimum is more than the maximum at other schools provided no reward or overt acknowledgement for simply achieving a standard higher than most other schools: going to class, showing up for school on time, being courteous, etc. Rather, I witnessed men and women being praised for achieving academically and socially beyond the minimum standards.

Obedience is evident in those who know and illustrate the true meaning of internal drive but internal drive is not found in obedience. Being obedient is most often described by a pet owner recounting the behavior of a "good" pet; a slave master describing his docile slave. Obedience is often developed from a fear of punishment or reprisal: obedience school for the dog; beatings with the whip for the slave. You are neither a pet nor a slave; are you?

The Future

Finally, to answer your question about what you should do in the future, I would expect you to realize that your future depends on you being all in – 100% of your total existence – and not even a pinky toe out. Either you share and support the "process" of your development unconditionally or you don't. There simply can be no in between. If you are to succeed, you must know that failure and quitting and the thoughts thereof are not an option. *As a man thinketh, so is he* (Prov. 23:7 King James Version). As you think, so are you.

In the future, you must understand what it really means to have internal drive. You must know that today while you vacillated about the road you should take, the spoken and unspoken words you uttered were those same words many unaccomplished, unfulfilled men have spoken.

I am referring to men who had the same potential as you who like you vacillated when they were challenged with fulfilling their destiny. At first those unaccomplished, unfulfilled men (and those responsible for their maturation) considered their utterances the mere words of a teen. However, the teens and the community soon discovered the power of words as those teens grew to be men who went on to waddle in disappointment, dismay and a depth of discontent I will not allow you to ever know.

Closing

Yes, I realize that you are "only" fourteen, soon to be fifteen. Yet, let me be perfectly clear though. While others may consider you a teen, to me you have always been my M.I.T, man in training. Hence, I don't subscribe to the same low expectations others have for you and those like you.

For me, the expectation is that from the moment you were born you have been matriculating to full manhood. In fact, my expectation is not unusual as in most places outside of the US, at your age, you would be expected to fend for yourself, your family and community. In many cases, fending for yourself and others would come with threats of extreme physical violence and the probability of death.

For me, treating you like a "teen", rather than expecting anything less than the exhibition of absolute manhood, is a parental contradiction that I believe is fraught with peril. Those who have a differing viewpoint – that you are just a teen – support a philosophy that I will never subscribe to.

For those who would hold you to anything less than a man, ask them how they would judge you if you were to do anything unlawful in this city, state or country. I am certain that they will not only accuse you as a man, they will judge you as a man, they will prosecute you as a man and they will sentence you for your crime as a man. And then you and I will have to visit and speak with one another as men from opposites sides of a glass window. You in an orange jumpsuit, shackled and residing on the side of the glass accompanied by all the other men who were allowed as "teens" to be confused about the roles and expectations of men. While I sat on the other side of the glass heartbroken by my failings as a father, mentor and friend.

As long as I am alive and kicking, you will never be confused about who you are or what is expected of you as a man. Moreover, I make you the promise that I will not make the same error that I made in having you prepared for today's meet or for life in general.

The choice is yours, you can get on board the ship to your success of your own free will and volition, or you can do so kicking and screaming. Either way, the journey to real manhood is not going to leave without you.

Dad

Questions

1. What's the difference between obedience and internal drive?

2. Why does the father apologize for being inadequate and failing his son?

3. Why does the father use the expression "As a man thinketh so is he"?

4. What expectations does the father have for his son?

5. What expectations do the adults in your life have for you? What expectations do you have for yourself?

6. What, according to the father, is the meaning of manhood?

Chapter 2: The Best Father's Day Ever!

Good evening National Qualifier:

It's funny when I look back on today. For starters, it is really good that I am writing you and not having an in person conversation. Man, I have no voice. I think that I may have to send you a doctor's bill for the treatment of laryngitis. Wait – that would be a waste of time; you don't have a job – you are still freeloading. I think my vocal chords are severely damaged from all the yelling and screaming – oops, I meant cheering and encouraging, I did today. Crazy parents yell and scream, civilized folks like me – well we cheer and encourage.

Second, my main man, I am as proud of you today as I have ever been. I'm so excited and encouraged about your future, and not just about you on the track. I am encouraged and excited about your future as a man. I saw something in you today that will carry you for the rest of your life.

The craziest thing about today is that we are both excited although our excitement is about different things. You're only nine, how could you have any idea about just how important today is towards the rest of your life?

I'm fairly sure that for you, today was a great day because you won a race that no one expected you to win, and you became the State/Regional Champion who will represent the State of Indiana at the USA Track and Field (USATF) Junior Olympics. Not to mention, today was a great day for you because you received a gold medal, which at this point in your life is a really big deal.

For me today was a much bigger day than witnessing you qualifying for Nationals, winning a couple of gold medals, or even being congratulated by all your family and friends. Don't get me wrong, all those things are really cool and important.

However, what really makes today special is that today was the realization, the proverbial proof in the pudding, that the hopes, plans and lessons you have been receiving on your road to manhood have not fallen on deaf ears. And while we are celebrating the proverbial proof in the pudding, let's add some icing on the cake. The icing on the cake for me is that all these good things occurred today, Father's Day.

As you well know, I am normally not without the words to express what I am thinking or feeling. Although I have some words, I simply can't articulate it enough: today was the culmination of so many of the things that I have talked to you ad nauseam about since the first day that I held you.

There were times, especially when you were an infant, that I wondered if you were too young to fully comprehend what I was trying to get you to understand. To be honest, there were times when I spoke to you as if you were a grown man, and those watching and listening thought that I was crazy.

Moreover, when you were a toddler, there were times when I wondered if you could appreciate any part of the significance and the urgency of the lessons that I was sharing with you. Again, those watching and listening to our conversations thought that I had flat out lost my mind.

What made today so great was that your efforts on the track told the story of a young man who understands, appreciates and has even begun to embrace the things that will allow him to reach his fullest God-Given potential. Another thing that made today really great was that I was able to stick my tongue out at the people who thought me crazy while exclaiming "nah, nah, nah, nah, nah…look who is crazy like a fox."

Years from now, I believe we will both look back on this day and realize that it was a seminal moment in your life. In other words, I believe today was one of your most important crossroads. You have two very different paths to choose: the path of least resistance or the path of the greatest personal sacrifice. These are two paths that you will encounter again and again throughout your entire life.

On this occasion, you chose the latter, which while imposing the greatest personal toll, it has also provided you with the greatest possible reward. Today you received the ultimate reward for that sacrifice.

One of the things that I most want you to remember about today is not the reward, or the results. I don't want you to focus on the bright shiny medal. I don't want you to focus on all the high fives, fist pumps, and pats on the back. I don't even want you to focus on the fact that you earned your way into your first Junior Olympics.

Instead, I want you to keep your attention on what truly matters, which is what was required to win the race. I want you to recognize that there is always a process for success.

Today's outcome was only possible because you had a process. As you will find with each new endeavor and experience you have, life will be more consistently enjoyable when you have and follow a process similar to the one that saw you leap into my arms for joy after winning your races today. In case you were not aware, the process that saw you succeed included passion, focus, seeking help and self-determination.

Passion

You ran with passion today; an unbridled joy, if you will. You were not only physically and mentally ready but it was as if your spirit was different from any other time that I can remember. You didn't just go through the motions; instead you ran as if you were in pursuit of something that you valued above any and all things. Today, my son, you ran your race as if your life depended on it.

Today's process will become increasingly more valuable as you get older. (I know, I know who wants to get older. Unfortunately, there is but one other choice and living and getting older is the much better option. Remember though, maturing doesn't mean you have to lose your childlike spirit.)

The difference between success and failure is far less about talent, and more about your passion. The more that you are willing to pursue your objective as if your life depended on it, the more often you will be successful. In the case of running, the more often you will be the victor. Always remember this: the greater the reward, the more passionate your effort must be.

Focus

You ran today with a single minded purpose. I originally thought the one thing on your mind was qualifying for the Junior Olympics. I realize now how absolutely incorrect that thought was. It appears that your greatest focus today was proving to all the doubters that you had not only what it took to qualify for Nationals but to beat their "predicted paper champion".

By the way, I spoke with Muhammad Ali and he told me that you are now the G.O.A.T., greatest of all time, and that you should go door to door to each of the naysayers singing "The Champ is here"! Okay, I know that was over the top but give me a moment to bask in the glow of your success. I am a proud papa. Okay the moment is over; back to my letter.

When you ran today, each pump of your arms and lift of your knees, accompanied a facial expression which told the story of a young man on a mission. It was almost as if you were possessed. Many great athletes call this possessed look, this uninterrupted focus being "in the zone". If you can find a way to bottle and reproduce the state of mind and demeanor from today, you will not only win a lot of races; you are going to be a winner at life.

Seek Help

I hope you always remember what you said you heard in your mind as you were running the competition down over the final 50 meters. Your words were *"I heard Coach Malone tell me to lift my knees and pump my arms"*. Years from now those exact words will carry less weight but the real value of those words, the first half of the sentence, will live forever. It is in the first part of the sentence that you acknowledged that sometimes in life we all need help. Sometimes we are best served when we look to those who know more than we do like Coach Malone, and simply ask for help.

The strength to seek help is a quality that you must continue to cultivate. Often men, young and old, struggle with asking for help. The fear is that asking for help says something unfavorable about them. This is a baseless notion and one that you should never adopt.

It is so important for you to understand that great men learn from other great people. Life is a minefield; like a real minefield there are places you should walk and there are places you should avoid. Only a fool would walk through life's minefields and not seek the guidance of those who had already walked through the minefield, and who knew where all the potential pitfalls, explosives and booby traps lay.

Do not ever be the man who is too proud or fearful to ask for help, because you will end up being the man who never sees his life fulfilled. You may also very well end up being the man who is missing limbs or sees his life cut short because he did not know where the pitfalls, explosives or booby traps lay. Whenever necessary, my son, seek help.

Self Determination

Say this out loud ten times: There is ABSOLUTELY NOTHING I CAN'T DO! In you, as it lies in all human beings, is the spirit to achieve and the capacity to be great. The unfortunate thing for the masses is that we doubt ourselves and our abilities continuously. We find every possible excuse so that we can skip giving our all and preparing for our lucky moment – where preparation and opportunity meet.

I'm too short, I'm the wrong color, I'm poor, etc. Even before we accept the challenge, even before we begin to prepare, most of us have already outlined, visualized, and defined all the reasons that we cannot succeed and thus have convinced ourselves that we should not even bother to make any effort.

Although you had every opportunity to do this, you didn't. Your reward was finishing in 1st place, winning your highly sought after Regional Championship medal, qualifying for Nationals, beating the competition and showing all the naysayers what happens when they doubt the heart of a champion.

Today your picture is listed in the dictionary under the words *self-determination*. Today, you determined for yourself what you could and would accomplish. You did not leave the outcome to the opinions or expectations of others. You were the master of your own fate; you were the captain of your own soul.

So now my main man, it is off to the SHIP, the USA Track & Field Junior Olympics National Championship. Now say that ten times. YES!

I can't predict the outcome but I do know that in you is everything you need to be everything you desire. More importantly, I know that you now know there is a process to having success at Nationals as well as in life. I'm not only ready for Nationals, but I am ready to see the man that you will soon become. Team Naeem all the way, baby.

Congratulations again!

Dad

P.S. In case I forgot to tell you, this was the best Father's Day ever.

Questions

1. What is meant by the path of least resistance and the path of the greatest personal sacrifice?

2. What are the four elements of "the process"?

3. How can "the process" help you and/or your child?

4. In this letter, the son is 9 years old. Do you think it's ever too early to start learning how to be a man?

5. What is meant by the use of the phrases "proof in the pudding" and "icing on the cake"?

6. Why is the father so excited and optimistic?

Chapter 3: Decide Right Now!

Naeem:

Your mom and I loathe coming to the games anymore…watching you sit, watching you make bad plays, watching less talented children play ahead of you, listening to folks whisper about you, etc. It's all so very depressing. And you know the worst part: it doesn't have to, nor should it be this way.

Our experience and feelings happen to be this way because you simply refuse to be CONSISTENT about your own success. You simply are not good enough to not do 30 minutes or more of foot skill drills each day. You simply aren't good enough not to strength train 3 times a week. You simply are not good enough not to work on your speed and agility at least 3 times a week. You simply are not good enough not to watch the video of the games I record for your benefit. You simply are not good enough not to study tactical formations. You simply are not good enough not to watch professionals. You simply are not good enough not to stretch properly after each game. You simply are not good enough not to do yoga twice a week or so. You are simply not good enough not to do mental psychological conditioning each day. What is most important for you to recognize is that you will never be good enough to not be CONSISTENT about your own success. In truth, no one is!

The best players, the great players, the players everyone idolizes…are those who do everything everyone else does at practice and significantly more than everyone else before and after games and practices. The players you say you want to be included with make NO EXCUSES about their success. These players let nothing or no one keep them from being successful. The groups that you are capable of belonging to don't sabotage their own success as you CONTINUE to do.

Your time is running out. You don't have all the time in the world to get what you want and believe you deserve. You are just going to have to decide how important your success is to you and at what price you are willing to pay.

Thus far your own SUCCESS doesn't seem too important and the price you are willing to pay is the "Dollar Store" equivalent.

Your raving but exhausted fan,

Dad

Questions

1. What are you willing to do to be successful?

2. Why is the father exhausted?

3. What does the son need to decide?

4. What does the father hope his son will learn about success and excuses?

Chapter Four: Dreams - The Pursuit of Happiness

Hey Soop:

I have been thinking a lot about you and your future, which should come as no real surprise to you or anyone who knows me, for that matter. Thinking about you and your future is the one thing that I have irrefutably done without hesitation or indifference since the moment that you were conceived.

Most recently, I have been thinking about how quickly time has elapsed. It seems like just the other day that you were small enough that I could lift you with just the palm of my hand – elevating you to heights that you thought were literally the highest in the world. Now you are much too large to hold in the palm of my hand and I find myself wondering how I can figuratively lift you up to unknown heights as I did when you were smaller.

This reflection has left me feeling anxious and concerned that I have not adequately prepared you for the future or as I define it that dreadful day when I can no longer stand literally by your side 24/7. I need you to know and understand, at this very moment in time, with complete clarity, that if I could make one request of you, it comes with my most sincere hope and prayer that when the time comes that you must do as all real men do – move out and establish your own existence – that you do so having followed your dreams.

As I get older or perhaps the better phrase is to say as I mature, I realize just how important it is to have a dream that wakes you each day, motivates and inspires you during the day, and that the effort and energy expended to accomplish that dream completely exhausts you each night so that you have a great night's sleep only to wake eagerly in the morning to do it all over again. This describes what being your father has been and meant to me.

Each and every day of your life, I have been excited to see you. I have been motivated and inspired by the thoughts of you, who you are and what you might become. I have gone to bed each night praying that your life is everything you could ever imagine, and that I could play some small part in the realization of your dreams even if my only role was simply not to mess things up for you.

My prayer for you always begins wishing that you triumph over that which I have yet to master myself, and that which your grandparents before you could not even begin to imagine mastering – dreaming and fighting to bring your dreams to realization. I do not believe your grandparents dreamt much of anything much less of greatness for themselves. While I have dreamt of greatness, I must be honest in telling you that I have at times lacked all the internal and external elements to make it happen – namely a direction, perseverance and support. In hindsight it now feels like much of my life, my own potential for greatness was squandered because I did not know how to follow and/or I simply failed to follow my own dreams.

I am telling you this now because I think you cannot only understand, but you should be able to appreciate fully the significance of my words. To be brief (which is not one of my greatest qualities), I don't want you to end up like me. I could quote all the well-known clichés that would hopefully inspire, motivate and drive home this point… "Don't put off tomorrow what you can do today" (Franklin n.d.) And "Tomorrow is not promised" (Matt. 6:34 King James Version).

Instead, I think the best thing that I can tell you is not to live your life with any regrets or misgivings. You need to know and understand that I am telling you this now because NOW is the time. In truth, NOW is all there ever has been, all there ever is and all there ever will be.

Life is made up of nothing more than billions of NOWS which are fueled and driven by our own individual dreams. If you miss acting NOW, you just might miss out on your dream. If you put off for later what you can and should do NOW, you just might put into motion actions that will change the course of your life and everything you have dreamt of.

I was watching the movie *Pursuit of Happyness* (The Pursuit of Happyness 2006) the other afternoon, and I watched one scene over and over again. It is the scene where Chris Gardner (played by Will

Smith) has a conversation with his son about dreams. The conversation went like this:

> Chris Gardner: *Hey. Don't ever let somebody tell you... You can't do something. Not even me. All right?*
> Christopher: *All right.*
> Chris Gardner: *You got a dream... You gotta protect it. People can't do somethin' themselves, they wanna tell you can't do it. If you want somethin', go get it. Period.*

What makes this scene so fascinating and significant is that Chris outlines for his son, Christopher, precisely what it takes to realize a dream. He tells him in step by step fashion exactly what to do. He delineates in this scene the instructions that every father should provide to his son in order that they may succeed in life.

First, implicit in his instructions is that his son MUST HAVE A DREAM and that he MUST ACT ON IT NOW. Christopher has a dream which he tells his father of just prior to the aforementioned dialogue. Christopher tells his dad while shooting hoops (preparing for his future while being in the now) that he is "going pro" (NBA). Unfortunately, Chris begins to discourage his son by focusing on his own lifetime of PAST personal failures until he catches himself and realizes that his failures do not have to be his son's failures. In fact, his PAST failures do not have to be a deterrent from the success of the NOW. I believe at that moment, Chris realizes that his PAST failures might instead provide a roadmap for not only his son's NOW, but both of their futures.

Second, the instructions infer that after you have discovered your dream, your passion and/or your purpose in life – you must resist any temptation to listen to anyone who would try to tell you that you cannot do something. Chris' statements confer that merely listening to negative, non-supportive comments even from those who you love and who love you are never allowable. Even as powerful as Chris' statement is it misses one very important and absolutely crucial consideration. What do you do when that "somebody who is trying to tell you that you can't do something" is you? In other words, how do you keep from letting your own negative thoughts impede you from achieving your dreams?

Negative thoughts that impact our ability to reach our dreams are known as Intrusive Thoughts. Intrusive thoughts much like the way Chris initially spoke to Christopher tell us in a multitude of ways why we can't and shouldn't try to do something. Intrusive thoughts leave us paralyzed to do those things that are required to make our dreams a reality such as prepare, practice, study, commit, and persevere. Intrusive thoughts cause us to obsess about our own shortcomings and make us view every bump in the road as an impenetrable fortress instead of what they really are – just an expected obstacle on the road to success. Intrusive thoughts make us focus not on improving our own status, abilities, or circumstances NOW and progressing towards the realization of our own dream NOW, but rather intrusive thoughts cause us to obsess over yesterday and tomorrow and the challenges of those whom we openly and/or secretly envy.

In order to achieve your dreams, you must go beyond acknowledging that there are those on the outside who do not believe in you, and want nothing more than to see you fail. More importantly, you must acknowledge that there is someone on the inside – your own actions, thoughts and behaviors – that might be keenly focused on seeing you fail. When you hear and/or see that person who would tell you that you cannot do something headed in your direction or looking at you in the mirror, you MUST NEVER TALK TO THEM.

Third, we learn that WE MUST PROTECT OUR DREAMS. This means that you must cover or shield your dreams from exposure, injury, damage, or destruction. You must nurture your dreams in the NOW. You should not associate yourself with anything or anyone who has the power to damage or destroy your dreams. Treat your dreams as if you're the parent of a newborn baby.

Your dream, just like the newborn baby, is powerless to survive without the parents' vigilant and unwavering attention and support. You are the unquestionable parent to your dreams. There is no DNA test required. Your thoughts were impregnated by your dreams. You birthed your dreams by your actions. Remember, it is up to you to nurture and care for your dreams so that they grow to their fullest potential. There are no social service agencies that step in to care for your dreams if and when you don't. If and when you stop caring for your dreams, they simply die.

Finally, we receive the last instruction which is IF WE WANT SOMETHING WE MUST GO GET IT PERIOD. Once you have dreamt the dream, you must NOW go get it. The dialogue does not say that you should have gotten it yesterday. Nor does the dialogue say that you should get it tomorrow. The dialogue says you must got get it, period, which clearly means in the RIGHT NOW.

Now, my dear son, is the time. How much do you want your dreams? I think the better expression would be to say IF WE NEED SOMETHING WE MUST GO GET IT PERIOD. How much do you need the realization of your dreams? How much do you need to take action NOW to make your dreams a reality?

For what it is worth, I believe the closer the dream is to a NEED rather than a WANT, the more likely you are to follow all the steps necessary to make it a reality. When your dream is like the thirst of a man stranded in the desert without water for three days, you will understand NEED and no one will ever have to tell you that you must go get it (your dream). If however, your dream is as it is for most people, simply the pursuit of dessert after an otherwise filling meal, you will never understand what it means to want or need something (your dream) so badly that you must go get it.

Now is the time, on this day, in this year, at this precise moment for you to determine if the fulfillment of your dream is akin to being in the desert dying of thirst, or are you just trying to decide between dessert and no dessert? The question is an important one and one that may determine the course of your life.

You have the instructions, the materials and the tools. At some point you will have to answer your own life's question: will my life be that of a man on his personal quest in the desert willing to die of thirst to realize his dreams, or will I be the man who goes through life trying to choose between dessert and no dessert?

Good luck and God Bless,

Dad

<u>Questions</u>

1. Why is it important to start pursuing your dreams now?

2. What are the four steps to pursuing your dreams?

3. When and how can we recognize intrusive thoughts?

4. Why should you avoid voices that speak negatively about your dreams?

5. What is the difference between a need and a want?

6. Why does the father compare dreams to needs instead of comparing them to wants?

Chapter Five: The Glass is ALWAYS Some Percentage of FULL

Dearest Naeem:

The other day when we were talking about how your day went, I mentioned that you should see the glass as half-full instead of half-empty. My suggestion was that you should find the positive out of the situation rather than focusing solely on the negative. In hindsight, I realize that my reply left something to be desired. I should have said something a bit more substantive and original instead of *"you should see the glass as half-full instead of half-empty"*.

It dawned on me after I noticed the look on your face that this tried and true expression may not have been one you were interested in trying, nor as I suspect did it ring true for you. Upon further reflection, I'm not even convinced that most people, especially those of us who utter this expression, including yours truly, interpret life and life's events this way.

Here I am attempting to inspire you, to keep you motivated when by the use of this expression, I might have done just the opposite. I uttered a commonly used expression without remembering that there is nothing common about you. You sir, are exceptional. As such, you deserve words and expressions that are comparable to you.

Forgive me for not having given any real thought about the expression previously, I will do so now. Now that I am thoroughly considering the expression, I can see why the mere utterance of the expression did not leave you looking overly convinced that the issues and concerns you raised were going to be resolved as you had hoped.

As I reflect on the expression, I find myself asking: What do we do when the glass is less than half full? Do we give up because the glass is more empty than full – concluding that the odds are not in our favor? What do we do when the glass is more than half full? Do we feel embarrassed, guilty and quit trying because while the odds have been in our favor we have not already accomplished the thing we are trying to accomplish? Perhaps these are the sort of questions and concerns that crossed your mind when you walked away from our conversation looking more perplexed than when our conversation began.

So now as a hip hop artist who changes the music and words of a pop, gospel or R&B song and watches as it becomes a hip hop hit, I am going to rephrase, I mean sample (hip hop lingo) the expression, *"see the glass as half-full instead of half-empty"*. I believe that this expression should be rephrased as follows: *"If there is anything in the glass then the glass is ALWAYS some percentage of FULL"*.

Hold your applause for now. I know I have skills. At the moment, I just need you to recognize my sampled expression is a better explanation of optimism.

Hopefully, now that I have sampled the expression, it is clear what I am intending to express to you. In short, I believe this rephrased expression is vital for you given the immense God-given ability that you possess, as it is so very critical that you never forget that it is always possible for you to do better, to do more.

If you are willing to have the faith and take the intellectual leap that is required when you see a half empty glass to perceive that the glass is also half full, why not go all the way and consider an almost empty glass as some percentage of full as well. To view the nearly empty glass this way is akin to a view of the world that acknowledges that all things are possible. As long as you have breath, desire, faith, second to none work ethic, and a willingness to succeed – you have a chance.

You will meet some people for which this way of thinking is unrealistic, but I believe that perception is an individual choice. What we perceive, and the way we interpret those perceptions, becomes our reality. We all have the option to see the world the way that we choose to see it. So I ask you, I challenge you, my son, to choose to see the world even when you consider things to be completely bleak as a glass with a drop of fluid – a glass that is some percentage of full.

If you are not yet a believer in my sampled version of the expression, I would encourage you to conduct a small science experiment tonight. After dinner, before you put your dishes in the sink or dishwasher, take a small amount of the scraps from your plate – something seemingly as innocuous as a piece of bread – and place it in an old glass (don't use a good glass or your mother will have a fit). The amount of scraps that you put in the glass should be so miniscule that you would be offended if someone offered you such a slight amount for dinner.

The point here is to illustrate that what often appears to be nothing can be just the beginning of something – a full glass. If you remember anything from chemistry, you know that in no time mold will begin to grow on the bread. You also might remember that if you leave the glass as it is (uncovered with the scraps still inside) before long the entire glass will be filled with mold. Not only will the glass be filled with mold but the room where the glass is located (which by the way will be your room as it is already like a large chemistry experiment) will smell like mold. Hence, a glass that once was thought to be empty will now be full.

While I have a doctorate degree it is not in science so this is where the chemistry lecture ends. However, it is important to note that the glass (which by the way is still in your room) will be filled with mold. If you put bread in the glass, you will have bread mold – a substance that is used to create penicillin. Penicillin is a drug that has been used to cure people of bacterial infections that were once fatal. Oh and that smell in your room means it is time to throw the glass away and wash your soccer uniform or throw out your shin guards...

Seriously, my real intention is not to get you to go purchase a Petri dish so that you can conduct your own science experiment. Rather my secret intent is to get you to clean your room. Okay, seriously at this moment, I want only to encourage you to remember that when something, even the smallest bit, exists in the glass, the glass ALWAYS has a chance to be FULL. In the same way, as long as you remain optimistic in the bleakest of times there is ALWAYS a possibility for a HAPPY ending and/or something MEANINGFUL to occur even when it was unimaginable.

So from now on, if you ever hear me or anyone utter the old expression, be sure to correct them and break them off with the new and improved hip hop sampled version. Despite what us old folks say, sometimes the new version can be better than the original, especially when the new version reminds us that we have a better than fifty percent chance of accomplishing our goals and realizing our dreams.

Deuces baby,

Dad

P.S. Jay-Z and Kanye have nothing on me.

Questions

1. Why does the father create an uncommon explanation for his son?

2. What expression does the father sample and what does the expression mean?

3. What does the father mean when he says that the "glass always has a chance to be full"?

4. Why is it important to be hopeful and optimistic as you pursue your dreams?

5. How is Penicillin created?

6. Why is our perception important?

Chapter Six: Goal Exercise #1, June 6, 2008

Naeem:

Write out a list of ALL the goals you wish to attain in soccer and track.

Prioritize them in order of importance and in relation to time. That is, label which are short term (up to 30 days), intermediate (4 - 6 months) and long term (a year and longer). Remember, intermediate and short term goals should lead you directly to and or be related to your long term goals.

Break the short term goals into smaller chunks by developing 2 to 4 mini goals or steps that you can take to help you reach these short term goals. Mini goals should be workable on a daily basis, in practice, or on your own

HINT: **Guidelines for Successful Goal Setting**

- Make sure your goals are CHALLENGING
- Make sure your goals are SPECIFIC. Vague and general goals like "I want to be faster or stronger" are not as helpful as "I want to run the 400 in 52 seconds" or "I want to juggle a soccer ball for 15 minutes nonstop."

- Make your goals MEASURABLE. You have to be able to specifically monitor your progress.

- Make your goals COMPATIBLE. A goal of wanting to juggle the ball like Ronaldinho is not compatible with reading Marvel Comics, listening to iTunes, or playing The Sims most of the day.

- Your goals should be FLEXIBLE to allow for CHANGES. If you set a goal too low, you need to be able to make the appropriate adjustment.

- Set a TIME FRAME or TARGET date for each goal. This time frame pressure will help you stay motivated towards completion. For example, "I will be able to juggle with all parts of my body nonstop for 15 minutes by August 1, 2008" or "I will run a 55 second 400 m by July 15, 2008".

- Put your goals in WRITING. Write down your goals, sign them and keep them continually in front of you (on your mirror, on your walls, in the car, at the kitchen table, etc.). This will help you make more of a commitment to working on them.

- PRIORITIZE your goals. Arrange your goals in relation to their importance and your long term objective

Recite this 10 WORD phrase over and over and over today (50 to 100 times) "IF IT IS TO BE, IT IS UP TO ME!"

Questions

1. What hints will you be able to use to start pursuing your goals?

2. Why does the father want his son's goals to be specific?

3. Why is the son instructed to put his goals in writing?

4. What does the phrase, "if it is to be, it is up to me" mean?

Chapter Seven: Goal Setting

Hey Soop:

There is something your mom, you, and I use to do at the beginning of each year. For no good reason, we stopped doing it. As I watch life pass us all by, like sand dripping from a near empty hour glass, it dawned on me that I had not given you enough tools to live the life you deserve.

How can you get where you want to go, if you don't know where you are going? How can you get where you want to go, if you don't have a map, directions, or a plan? How will you even know if you get to the right destination without some prior contemplation and strategy for the desired course of your life?

With that said, I want; no I need you to give some thought about a few highly important, potentially life altering questions: (write your answers down as we will create a living, breathing plan)

1. What would you like your life to be in 10 years from now?
    a. What will be your occupation?
    b. What will you have accomplished from now through 2020?
    c. Will you still be playing soccer?
        i. If so, at what level?

d. Will you still be running track?

    i. If so, at what level?

e. Will you continue to value education?

    i. If so, what level of formal education will you have completed or be in pursuit?

f. What will people say, think, and feel about you? (Friends, family, general public)

g. What will your financial status be?

h. What will your standard of living be? (Home, car, savings, etc.)

2. What will your life look like in 2013 (the day you graduate from high school), if the life you desire in 10 years is to be a reality?

    a. What will you need to be doing to be on target to fulfilling your 10 year plan?

    b. What will you have already accomplished during high school to stay on track to making your 10 year plan a reality?

Now let's sit down together and develop some real, measurable, and tangible goals that will help you stay the course to playing the STAR role in your life instead of what most of us do which is to play a supporting CAST member at best. Often times, we simply play an extra, which is pathetic - to not have more control of OUR OWN LIFE.

I owe you better than to let you repeat my errors. I owe you more than not making sure you live a more enriched, satisfying, accomplished life than me. I don't have much to give you, but perhaps my greatest legacy to you can be making certain that you have a plan, that you have a focus, that you have a commitment, that you have passion and direction for having the life you were DESTINED to live.

Let's get to work. Unfortunately, time waits for no one...not even you, my beloved and only begotten son.

Wishing you the greatest life possible,

Dad

<u>Questions</u>

1. What will your life look like 10 years from now?

2. What steps can you take today to make that dream a reality?

3. Everyone leaves a legacy. What legacy have your parents left you?

4. What would you like people to say about you in 10 years from now?

Chapter Eight: The Green Sea Turtle

Hey Soop:

As usual, I had a great time hanging out with you in Brazil. Generally, wherever you are is where I want to be as well.

Was it surreal or what - to finally be in the country where you have admired the greatness of its National soccer team and romanticized what it would have been like to have grown up playing soccer there? The home of Pele, Ronaldo, Rivelino, Socrates, Ronaldinho, and the list of Brazilian soccer greats just goes on and on. There were so many other memorable things about our time in Brazil that will live in my memory forever. I will never forget our visits to the Desportivo Brasil (your future home), the Museu do Futebol, our visit to ABC FC, our visit to the dunes of Natal, our visit to the beach of Ponte Negra, the four hour dune buggy ride, ...or the women in Brazilian (thong) bikinis (Bye the way, I think that we should keep that part of the trip to ourselves even if you are now seventeen).

There was one particular sight on the beach that I want to bring to your attention. No I don't care how much you try to twist my arm; this is not where we are not going to talk about all those Brazilian women walking around in thongs. Get your mind right young man! What would your mother say if she read this letter or read your mind for that matter?

Seriously, the creature on the beach that I want to talk about that I believe is worth closer inspection is non-other than the Green Sea Turtle. Yes son, I want to talk to you about a turtle. Not just any turtle though, the Green Sea Turtle.

Relax, my man, and trust me, if you are going to spend a year in Brazil we are going to have plenty of opportunities to talk about thongs, the women who wear them, and a whole lot of other "birds and bees" stuff. However, for now, I just want to talk about the Green Sea Turtle, if that is alright with you.

Now that I think about it, I'm not even sure that you noticed the Green Sea Turtle while we were on the beach. The morning I left the hotel early to work out on the beach, I saw a Green Sea Turtle and I knew almost immediately that it would serve as a profound subject matter for a future discussion.

Your pending journey to Porto Feliz is going to be reminiscent of the life and times of the Green Sea Turtle. Sometimes the turtle swims where the tide is high; sometimes it swims where the tide is low. Similarly, you will experience physical highs like being unstoppable on the field – able to weave through, in and out, and around opponents with the ball as it were tied to your shoe laces. At other times, you will experience physical lows like being unable to tie your shoes and chew bubble gum concurrently. (Well let's hope your lows never reach that level but if by some unfortunate chance they do, consider yourself forewarned).

There are times when the Green Sea Turtle swims on the water's surface and then there are other times when it disappears well beyond sight as it descends to the furthest depths of the ocean. In the same way, there may be times when your spirits will be up for the entire world to see. During those high moments, it will feel as though your mind and body are in perfect tune. Any thought you have will seem to be magically and almost simultaneous manifested in your actions and abilities. Again there may also be times when your spirits are low – reflecting a total disconnect between your mind and body. During these times, your mind and body will behave as if they speak totally different languages: the body speaking in English; the mind speaking in Portuguese. The two will even appear to be going in opposite directions: the body North; the mind South.

Like the Green Sea Turtle who spends most of its life submerged in water, your life submerged in soccer for the next year will undoubtedly be filled with highs & lows and ups & downs. I hope this letter does not come across as intent to scare you or suggest in any way that you are unprepared. Quite the contrary! I just want you to remember that life's journey is never flat, if it were so you would never know the joys of victory or the agony of defeat. Life, my benevolent son, will always be filled with highs and lows; ups and downs.

The reality, I trust, is that we both know that there will be moments where things seem a bit scary and you feel unprepared. I'm telling you now in advance; don't worry about any of that. After watching the Green Sea Turtle stick its neck out, dive to unbelievable depths in the ocean, resurface and do it all again, I am convinced that this routine is simply how life should and has to be experienced. If the Green Sea Turtle can take chances, do the unthinkable, return to start, follow the same routine over and again and not only survive but thrive, you as one of God's creatures who reside at the top of the food chain have to be in a great position to enjoy the same or better life than the Green Sea Turtle.

Come Out of Your Shell

Since you didn't see the Green Sea Turtle, I want you to know that, for the most part, it is similar to most other turtles. It possesses a hard exterior, a shell. The shell while serving to protect turtles can also put turtles in grave danger. In essence, the shell is both a blessing and curse to the turtle. The shell can protect the turtle from predators and dangerous objects. However, hiding in the shell for an extended period of time could also keep the turtle from life affirming things such as finding food, connecting with family and friends, as well as avoiding any predator that is powerful enough to destroy them regardless of their shell.

As you prepare mentally, physically and emotionally to be on your own, you would be well served to keep the Green Sea Turtle in mind. There will be times when it will be best for you to protect yourself by covering yourself in your own shell. Avoiding idle, useless, or disrespectful conversation and activity would qualify as times when being in your shell would be appropriate. However, be mindful if you have to retreat to your shell to not to stay in your shell for too long, as you will undoubtedly miss out on something that is important. Moreover, if you retreat to your shell too long, you might even miss out on an opportunity to be the catalyst for correcting behavior and/or conversations that would otherwise be deemed inappropriate or disrespectful. Retreating in your shell for too long might cause you to miss the opportunity to meet and share experiences with those who share similar goals, dreams and desires as you. Retreating too long might have the ill-timed and ill-intended effect of causing you to basically miss out on life. In sum, life simply cannot be lived when you are hiding in a shell. Hide if protection is an absolutely necessity; otherwise, by any means necessary, please stick out your neck.

Stick Out Your Neck

While watching the Green Sea Turtle last week, I noticed that when the turtle made up its mind about the direction that it wanted to go, it stuck its neck out of its shell as far as possible and then proceeded to make its way towards its destination with urgency and conviction. There was no partial sticking out of the neck. There was no inch by inch, looking around cautiously and then lengthening the neck another inch or so. There was no peek-a-boo behavior – repeatedly extending and extracting the head in and out of the shell in some uncertain manner.

Instead, the turtle seemed to extend its neck with one predetermined motion as far as physically possible. As a matter of fact, it appears that the furthest extension of the neck was a physical and mental mandate for the turtle. To do other than give a full and complete extension left the turtle with limitations on its peripheral view which was caused by the length, width and depth of the shell. It appears that without full neck extension the turtle would have limitations on its ability to find food, to avoid predators and to be able to connect with family and friends. Evidence once again that as useful as the shell can be, it can also be a hindrance to participating fully and enjoying all the wonderful aspects of life.

In your upcoming journey, you are going to have to mimic the behavior of the Green Sea turtle. There will be times that you are simply going to have to be bold and have faith – there will be times when you will have to stick your neck out as far as possible regardless of the potential risks and fears (such as failure and embarrassment) if you are going to move forward and go as deep as you can go in your pursuit of soccer excellence. Like the Green Sea turtle, you are going to have to not only stick your neck out, but you are going to have to do so well beyond your comfort level, without reservation or trepidation. The new adventures that await you-striving to accomplish your dreams, maximizing your fullest potential - will all be negatively impacted and severely limited if you choose to do anything other than extend your neck as far as humanly possible, and immerse yourself totally in every aspect of the environment which includes: eating, breathing and sleeping.

Breathing and Sleeping

Okay, so I will admit that in order to write this part of the letter, I had to do some research in advance. In full disclosure, once we returned home, I Googled Green Sea Turtles. Go ahead make your jokes about my proclivity for doing research. I can't help it; it is just a part of who I am. At any rate, Smart Alec, the research about the Green Sea Turtle provided one additional tidbit of information that I believe is not only similar to, but beneficial for, your forthcoming journey.

Are you ready for the mesmerizing tidbit of information? Green Sea turtles spend almost all their lives submerged. Ah ha! I bet you didn't know that. I bet you are thinking what's the big deal? The big deal is that the Green Sea Turtles spend almost all their lives submerged. Put another way, the Green Sea Turtle spends almost all its life immersed in the environment that provides both all of its needs as well as it greatest dangers.

Soon your environment, the environment you will reside in will be much like that of the Green Sea Turtle's. The environment will not only be a place that feeds you mentally, physically and emotionally, but it will also be the place of life's daily challenges and difficulties both on and off of the field. Son, like the Green Sea Turtle, immerse yourself immediately in your environment. Give everything you have, give every ounce of your being; even give the essence of your soul to the environment that can make your life long dreams a reality.

Don't spend even one second trying to find other places to surface. Don't take any mental journeys or vacations that take you away from your environment. Stay present and in the moment at all times: mentally, physically and spiritually. Don't give a thought to what is going on any place other than where you are.

Do you think the Green Sea Turtle could survive at the depth of the ocean if it were thinking also about crawling on the sand? If you are going to be what you want to be and do what you want to do, you must at all times stay completely and fully immersed in the environment that will help you reach all your goals and objectives.

I know; who knew that there was so much to learn from a turtle? Who knew when we arrived in Brazil that a turtle would provide a path on how to survive and thrive while you are away? FOX has a TV game show that asks the question, are you smarter than a fifth grader. I'm going to ask the question, are you, Naeem, smarter than a Green Sea Turtle? I believe you are, but only time will tell for sure.

The Green Sea Turtle has shown that it has this surviving and thriving thing all figured out. I have a sneaky suspicion that you can figure it out as well. Who knows with all the ridiculous shows on TV, maybe FOX will develop a show that pits you against the Green Sea Turtle.

If I had to place a bet on your understanding and preparedness about surviving and thriving as compared to the Green Sea Turtle, I would do so in a heartbeat. Just to be clear though, you better not let me down. It's bad enough not to be as smart as a fifth grader, but I can't be losing any of my hard earned money to a stinking Green Sea Turtle.

Luv ya later!

Dad

Questions

1. What life lessons can we learn from a Green Sea Turtle? Are there any other animals from which we can learn? Which ones?

2. Describe the times when you have been stuck in your shell?

3. How can you be present, in the moment, at school? At work? Playing sports?

4. What does the father believe will occur if his son sticks his neck out?

5. What is meant by being submerged in your life?

6. How can you be fully committed to your dreams?

Chapter Nine: Instant Message with Naeem – Growing Pains

Poot says: Hi dad how are you?

Poot says: How was your day?

Poot says: ?

The Smooth One says: Let me check...BEAUTIFUL!

The Smooth One says: How are you?

Poot says: IM OK

The Smooth One says: Why just ok?

Poot says: I guess mom hasn't told you

Poot says: I'm getting an incomplete in Spanish

The Smooth One says: Told me what?

Poot says: *incomplete

The Smooth One says: Are you in trouble again?

Poot says: No it's just my Spanish teacher is giving me an incomplete for this nine weeks because the video for the project didn't work and mom got mad at me

The Smooth One says: So does that mean the whole group gets an incomplete? Will she allow you the opportunity to make it up?

Poot says: Yes, the whole group does
Poot says: And I'm not really sure

The Smooth One says: So what did the group have to say to you?
The Smooth One says: I'm sure that they are pissed at you.

Poot says: Nothing because I just found out we didn't have time to play the video in class
Poot says: See you're mad at me too

The Smooth One says: Did I say anything about being mad at you?

Poot says: No, it just it seems like it

The Smooth One says: How does it seem like it? Where did I write anything that sounded like I was mad? I think you are internalizing things and placing your feelings on me.

The Smooth One says: All I did was ask a couple of questions.

Poot says: I'm sorry dad I'm just a little crazy right now

The Smooth One says: Crazy?

Poot says: No
Poot says: I mean over emotional

The Smooth One says: Well what you are experiencing is what many other men have experienced. It is called growing pains. You want more responsibility. You want more credit. You want people to believe in you more than ever. Unfortunately, with all those wants comes a lot of work. This is something you are learning and will continue to learn

Poot says: Ok

The Smooth One says: I went through it. Uncle Willie went through it. All men go through it. Things will never be like they were when you were a kid. The more you move toward full manhood, the more people will expect you to behave like a man. Since you are not Peter Pan, all you can do is prepare yourself for the inevitable. The better prepared you are, the easier life will be.

Poot says: Ok, thank you

The Smooth One says: My pleasure. That is what GOOD fathers do! One day you will have the same conversation with your son because like you feel right now, he will feel like he can't do anything right. You can tell him what I am telling you...it is a rite of passage into being what you have been wanting to be from birth, a MAN!

Questions

1. What are growing pains? How often have you experienced them?

2. What is a rite of passage that you have in your family or community?

3. How do you handle frustration? Disappointment?

4. What role models do you have that can give you good advice?

Chapter Ten: It's Not Too Late

Hey Naeem:

I just wanted to take a brief moment to say a few things to you. And yes, I know you will find this surprising, but I do know how to be brief. Okay, so here goes my attempt at brevity!

The first thing that I want to say is one thing that I could never possibly tell you enough. I love you man! Yes, I said it. If after all these years, you are not yet use to hearing me say those three short but distinct words, get accustomed to it. No matter how old you get, how muscular and strong, or how manly you become, I will always be the father who yells those three short but distinct words from the bottom of the valley to the top of the mountain for all the world to hear.

"I love you man". There I said it again. You should know that I have loved you from conception and will do so until the end of time.

Second, I want to tell you how much I appreciate you. I am certain that like many other parents, I have not done this adequately enough. I appreciate who you have been, all that you are now and who I expect that you will become. It has been an undeniable honor and a pleasure to serve as your mentor, father and friend.

When asked about my relationship with you, I answer by saying what I most like about you. I tell them that while you have not been a perfect child, you have been a perfecting child. In other words, I tell them that you have done the one thing that I believe all parents would and should ask of their children – not that they are the best at everything they attempt, but instead that they give their best effort in any and all things that they have endeavored. I believe that I can unequivocally say that you have done this. Thank you for respecting your time, talent and opportunities by being prepared to give your best effort whenever you were called upon to do so.

Thirdly, and probably most important, at least for today, I want to say thank you for giving me some food for thought – some needed words of encouragement – for strengthening me when I was weak. I can't stress strongly enough the significance of your words. I do not take your wise declarations or your keen insight for granted.

Psalms 8:2 has a quote that speaks to wisely identifying that children often possess the ability to say life altering things. "Out of the mouth of babes and sucklings thou hast found thy strength…"(Psalms 8:2 King James Version). The point of this verse is that the power of God does not make itself known only when human beings have reached full adult development, but that even from infancy babies possess such power as to articulate reverence for and celebrate God. If this quote is true, and I believe that it is, then it goes without saying that you possess the ability to articulate the words to your own father, which can not only strengthen him, but your words can also move him to have a greater reverence for his own life, and to motivate him to live his life as an active celebration, and not as a predetermined obituary.

Not only do I respect and appreciate what you say verbally, but I have often found that even when I write you, it is as if I feel your presence and response to my words in a spiritual nonverbal capacity. As such, I have learned to reflect on the words that I write to you, as they have become unintended messages for me. The letters to you have become a call of action for me, and hopefully you have benefitted from them as much as I am now benefitting from them.

So a few weeks ago when we spoke about following your dreams, you said to me, *"Dad, it is not too late for you, you can still follow your dreams"*. These words have stayed with me continuously the last several days. *"Dad, it is not too late..."*

I am almost embarrassed to say this to you, but the unfortunate truth of the matter is that despite all the ways that I try to inspire you to be encouraged about your future, I have simply considered my life for all practical purposes to be over. No, I don't have some life threatening disease or illness, but I did consider that I had accomplished all that I was ever going to accomplish with my life and anything to be applauded from this day forward would be accomplished exclusively by you.

I suppose in a way that I was simply thinking that I would just bide my time until my breathing ceased. I would be like just any other of the tens of millions of American adults who get up aimlessly every day, go off to work, come home and do it all again. Yes, your dad had resigned himself to being one of the walking – talking adult American Zombies. If this portrayal appeared in a movie, I would be the corpse of a man who had no idea that he was in fact already dead, but was nonetheless aimlessly moving about the earth with no real purpose or direction. This is the sad but real existence of so many, including your father. This is the precise existence that I have always wanted and needed you to avoid.

Your words reminded me that this is a horrible way to approach life. In fact, this is completely contrary to anything that I would expect of, or allow, from you. Yet until you said *"**Dad it is not too late...**"* this is precisely how I had been approaching life. Who knew...your dad, The American Zombie?

So again thanks! Thanks for doing as you have done for everyday that you have inhabited the earth – inspire and encourage me to be a better man. From this day forward, my promise to you is that I am going to keep your words close to my heart and mind. I am going to stop sleep walking through this life and live it with the same energy and passion that I expect you to live your life. I am going to do those things that I am passionate about to my fullest potential and ability, the same way I expect you to do. I am going to believe in the possibility of dreams and accomplishing those dreams, even at my advancing age. Finally, I am going to live my life with real purpose and direction – I am going to develop a living breathing written tangible life plan that I can follow so as to never become one of the American Zombies again.

Out of the mouth of my son, I heard the profound words that have changed my life – "***Dad, it is not too late for you, you can still follow your dreams***." Thank you son for speaking truth to me. Through your words I have found the courage and the strength to be the same man that I want you to become.

If it is okay with you, I would like to be a better man too – a man equal to the man I realize that my son has already become.

Thanks so very much!

Dad

Questions

1. In this chapter, the father says that the son has inspired him to not give up on his dreams, even though he is already an adult. Do you believe that dreams have an age limit, why or why not?

2. How can you be an inspiration to the people around you, even the adults in your life?

3. Who are the American Zombies? How does one become an American Zombie? How does one avoid becoming an American Zombie?

4. Should more parents look to their children for inspiration and motivation?

5. Do you or your parents have dreams that you have not followed?

6. Have you considered developing a life plan so that you don't lose your way like the father?

Chapter Eleven: It's Not Where You Start, but Where You Finish

Hey Soop:

I hate to be the one to give you this news but unfortunately, or fortunately depending on your perspective, you need to know that there will be times when you will be the worst person on the field, the slowest person on the track or the least accomplished person in the classroom. I'm going to assume you think that I just delivered bad news. In actuality, this is really nothing but good news.

How can being the worst, slowest, or least accomplished be described as good news, you ask? I'm so glad that you asked. Well my young king, all three of these scenarios provide you with a chance to do only one thing: IMPROVE. Being at the bottom provides you with a good fortune that those at the top do not have. Those already at the top can only go one direction…DOWN!

When you are at the bottom there is only one direction that you can go, and that direction is up! There is no sub-bottom for you to reach. If there was a sub-bottom you would not be at the bottom.

Let me pause for a second now so that I can ask you a question. Are you as excited about receiving this news as I am about giving it? If not, you should be. Okay, if you are, or if you are not, pay attention anyway. I promise, before I'm done you will share my excitement.

I suspect that if you are not already excited that you have forgotten what I have been stressing to you for years now, which is that life can only be lived in the present. You cannot live for yesterday, and you cannot live for tomorrow. When I say living, I hope you remember that I mean "living", and not the thing most people do…exist. Living means simply being present in the only moment that matters: the moment that you are in. When you live in the present moment you will know it, as you will give no thoughts to yesterday, and you will have no concerns about tomorrow.

When you live life like the masses you will spend your time focusing on what happened yesterday, and what you hope happens tomorrow. When you live life like the masses, you will spend your time focusing on the Goal and the End Result, without realizing that the goal cannot be accomplished, and that the end result cannot be achieved, if you don't do what you need to do at this very moment, the PRESENT.

The process for living in the moment that you can use to matriculate on the road of success is simple. It's a three part process. I call it the ABC's of success.

A stands for Admission. You have to admit that you are at or near the bottom. It's okay! If you are the least skilled player, admit it. Everyone else knows it already anyway, so there is no value in lying to yourself. You are not a fool so don't act like one by trying to trick yourself into believing that you are something or somewhere other than who you are or where you are.

A does not stand for Acceptance. You don't have to accept your current ranking or station. You simply have to acknowledge, admit where you are. Otherwise, you are like a man lost at sea who is either too dumb or stubborn to admit that he is lost. He doesn't know how to get home and no one knows where he is. This is the text book definition of lost.

However, until he acknowledges that he is lost and sends out an SOS call, no one can get his coordinates so that he can be saved. Once he is rescued, he can continue his journey, but if he doesn't admit that he is lost, in all likelihood he is going to die alone at sea. Don't be like the man lost at sea. Be completely honest with yourself, admit where and who you are. Then you can place your SOS call and there will be someone – a coach, a teacher, a parent – capable of helping you to make your journey a success.

B stands for Belief. You have to simply believe that you can accomplish your goal or achieve your desired end result. In either case, you have to believe. How do you believe you can accomplish something, when you currently are the worst, slowest and/or least accomplished? Simple, you reflect on a time when you were not the worst, slowest and/or least accomplished. You turn your attention to a time when you were the best, fastest and/or most accomplished. This, by the way, is the only time when you are allowed to consider the past. The past is only relevant when it serves not as a place where we will live and choose to be stuck in, but only as a reminder of our great potential.

If the journey is something so ambitious that it cannot be compared to anything in your past, let me take a moment to first say congratulations. In case you did not know this already, the world only progresses when people really dream – when people move far beyond their comfort level. Now using one of the pieces of technology that you own (mobile phone, laptop or tablet) that were invented by someone just like you who dreamt of doing something others most likely thought impossible, Google "people who achieved greatness despite great obstacles". Here you will find people who started at the bottom, people who came from not just humble-but meager-beginnings. People who had physical limitations that went on to do just what they dreamt about doing, and sometimes much more. Surely, if others who have started from zero, who started from places of desolation, who started with physical impairments, could achieve their dreams and accomplish their desired end result, how much more can you possibly achieve?

C stands for commitment. This is the final part of the triad for success, and the most difficult. You will find that this third part is the most difficult because most people do not know how to commit to anything. As an example, millions of Americans make New Year's resolutions that do not last beyond the first month of the year.

Instead of losing the weight we resolve to lose we get fatter. Instead of reducing the debt that we resolve to decrease we instead make new purchases on our credit cards the moment we learn about the New Year's Day sale. Such is the way most people commit; by not committing at all. It is possible that the majority define commitment differently – resolving to do the things that we know will keep us from achieving our goals and resolutions.

So that you do not end up like the masses, you must understand what the word commit actually means. To commit means that you are bound and/or obligated to do something. You are bound and/or obligated to do the thing that you said you were going to do – the one thing that you said was of the utmost importance.

If you say that you are going to lose ten pounds in the New Year, then you are bound to lose all ten. Losing nine and a half pounds won't do. If you say that you are going to pay off your credit card then you are obligated to do so. Paying off ninety nine percent of your balance is not acceptable.

When you are bound you are stuck, you can do nothing except be bound. When you are obligated you are trapped, you can do nothing less than fulfill the obligation in its entirety. This is a condition of commitment that will have you advancing down the road of success in no time.

As simple as this may sound, few are able to do this. Actually, I should have said, few are willing to follow through with the things they resolve to do. Ordinarily, the person who resolves to lose ten pounds follows the process to lose weight for the first couple of days, and before they can see any significant results, return to their last year, get fat and sick, dietary routine. In no time, the person has gained an extra five or ten pounds, and now needs to lose fifteen to twenty pounds which they, of course, will not commit to lose until next New Year.

The same can be said of the person who resolves to get out of debt. They see an advertisement for a big screen TV that can be purchased same as cash, interest free for ninety days. They purchase the TV and ninety days later – you guessed it – after making only the minimum payments they have increased their debt. As it is with the person resolving to lose weight, they will do nothing to decrease their debt until next New Year's resolution.

These people fail to understand that there is a reason why the expression is the "road to success". Success is a journey and not a destination. Success requires that you take a step in the right direction each day. Success requires that you do something to get you where you are attempting to get each and every day.

If you are attempting to lose weight, successful weight loss requires that you eat fewer calories and/or burn additional calories each and every day. If you are attempting to get out of debt, successful debt reduction requires that you stop purchasing depreciable items and/or make additional payments on your existing debt each and every day. Thus, each day that you do something that advances you during your journey; this is success. In the words of Ice Cube, when you do the aforementioned, you can end the day by singing "today was a good day" (O. Jackson 1992).

It is important to note that people are successful at times in their lives, not all the time; no one is successful all the time. However, the trick is to have more moments of success than moments of disappointment. Those that have significantly more moments of success are those who have mastered the art of commitment. These are the folks who understand how to bind and obligate themselves to their journey.

You too must master binding and obligating yourself to your journey. This part, binding and obligating yourself, should be easy as it is biologically engrained in you at this particular stage in your life. This is the one time for you to totally embrace your teenage narcissism.

Yes, I know this line of thinking is contradictory to everything adults try to tell you at this stage in your life, but if you are going to progress on the road of success in the expeditious and efficient manner that you desire, you are going to have to channel your inner teenage narcissist.

This is the time when you must put your hopes and dreams first, and not worry about the collective. This is the time when you must expend all your available time and energy on resolving to do those things that move you down the road of success. This is the time for you to do everything in your power to do whatever is humanly possible to reach your goal and/or achieve your end result.

These are the ABC's of success, my son. This is the prescription for moving you from out of the outhouse and into the penthouse. These are the directions for moving you out of the basement and up to the rooftop balcony. You never, never ever, have to stay the worst, the slowest or the least. Remember, should you ever find yourself in the worst, slowest, least situation, all you have to do to change your position is admit, believe and commit.

If you can do just these three things, you are going to pass – on the road to success – many a person who were once considered better, faster and more "whatever" than you. If you are able to do these three things on your road to success, you will find fewer speed bumps, potholes and detours. If you will do these three things you will find your journey more often paved a road of gold.

To nothing but your success,

Dad

Questions

1. The father outlines a path to success that he calls the ABCs of success. What part of the path is the most important? Why?

2. What does the acronym ABC stand for?

3. Who are "the collective" and why does the father want his son to never pay attention to them?

4. In this chapter, the father allows the son to use the past as a reference – why?

5. What does the father want his son to know about New Year's resolutions?

6. Have you ever considered quitting something because you were not the best?

Chapter Twelve: Just Compete!

Naeem:

The following is an excerpt from an article that I read the other day. I believe the author clearly lays out things that you must never stop doing if you are going to have the type of success athletically, academically, and eventually professionally that you desire.

"In early September, there was a Division I game between two Top Ten teams, one from the West Coast and one from the East Coast. It was an early season special. Two big time programs went at each other; each hoping to make a statement for the 2008 collegiate season. It was a beautiful day and the stadium was full. After observing the game for the first half, it was clear that the West Coast team had better soccer players. Pound for pound they were more technical than the home team. The West Coast team lost 3-0 - and it could have been more. Good soccer players; who played good soccer but didn't compete. They PLAYED the game; they did not COMPETE the game.

In a recent interview discussing the upcoming NHL season, Columbus Blue Jackets (CBJ) coach Ken Hitchcock told reporters that the CBJ would make the playoffs if he could find players "who would COMPETE and not just PLAY". And, there is a difference he said. "Players who PLAY bring skill; players who COMPETE bring everything!"

There is too much playing in American soccer and not enough competing. Playing permeates all levels of the game from Underage 5 (U5) to the MLS and the National teams. We are confusing ability for talent. As Allen Fox, author of The Winners Mind suggests, "Most people mistake speed and skill for talent. Real talent STARTS with energy, drive, work ethic and the will to win. Without these attributes, a player can never be great."

In this country we have focused so much on playing, that we have not taught our players to compete - to fight - to work hard or to have the will to win. As a soccer culture, we have always had an inferiority complex. So, we emphasize playing, technical ability and skills. Our youth players play a lot of soccer, but few compete." (Empire United Soccer Academy 2013)

The points that the author made in this article could not have been said better even by me. The only difference is that he was writing it to an unknown audience and I am sending it to you, my SUPAMAN. YOU have the ability to do whatever your mind can conceive of you doing. You simply must learn and never stop competing.

Everyday life requires you to compete. Don't ever settle for existing. Don't ever settle for just being on the field or sitting in the classroom. ALWAYS and I do mean ALWAYS, COMPETE.

If you COMPETE, when you COMPETE, you will find that those players who want you to think that they are the stars, those students who think they are the class geniuses...they will fold like a bad hand of poker. Those players/students lack the motivation and confidence to COMPETE. The minute you make it a bit of a challenge, the minute things are no longer easy, they give up. There is not a soccer player who will be on the field with you tomorrow at Olympic Development Program (ODP) or any Underage 14 (U-14) player in the country who can out COMPETE you. Not one! The only player who can out COMPETE you is YOU!

When competing is measured correctly, the focus is on effort rather than ability. The world is replete with people who have great ability but render little to no effort. Check the graduation photos of kids all over the country who finished high school with honors but never earned a college degree. Look at the record books of all the highly rated high school athletes that never earned a college degree or played professional sports. Look at the records of kids who had perfect SAT scores yet fail to contribute to society. The difference in their success or failure in many of those cases was their willingness, their desire to COMPETE.

Competing in soccer and on the track is as much an indication as your ability and willingness to COMPETE in life. Every day, you either work or you get outworked. It is just that simple! YOU must COMPETE!

The good thing for you is that you know what it means to COMPETE. You have historical evidence to draw strength from:

You qualified for your 1st Junior Olympics (JO) by COMPETING. You beat a cocky, slightly taller sprinter who was expected to win the State/Regional Title. You ran him down from 50 -75 meters out. You ran him down because you COMPETED. You ran him down because you had HEART and DESIRE. You ran him down because COMPETING was more important than winning. After that race, like most bullies, he never beat you again.

You nearly single handily defeated the entire Dynamo team when you played for the Burn. That day you were all over the field, taking the ball from any and all Dynamo players. You led all the offensive attacks that the Burn had that day. When your teammates were too tired to get back on defense, you played the whole back by yourself. You were a man possessed that day. You were a man who was COMPETING. That day surrendering to the Dynamo teams was not an option. That day playing like your hair was on fire was your non-verbal statement – I will compete. That day the parents of the privileged, egotistical children took notice of the one guy who competed. That day the coach who once said "he only played his best players at the end of the game" came to shake your hand to tell you how good you were and how he would like for you to come back and play for his club. That day you understood that technical skill is one thing but HEART and the ability to COMPETE are what makes real champions. The Burn did not win that game but everyone knew who COMPETED – you.

During the 4 x400 meter relay at the Junior Olympics (JO) in Indianapolis, your teammate passed you the baton for your anchor leg. You received that baton 100 m behind the next competitor and you were in last place. I remember you telling me, "Dad I saw that guy and I was not going to finish last". Without defining what you did on that day, at that moment, you decided to COMPETE. You ran that guy down and finished before him by 40 m. You COMPETED in that race. The fact that your team was not going to qualify for the finals was of no consequence. What was important to you was that you showed enough HEART, DESIRE, and DETERMINATION to never give up. You COMPETED to the very end – all the way through the finish line.

At this year's, Amateur Athletic Union (AAU) Nationals when your 4 x 400 m team took the track, you were the only member to COMPETE. You were the only member to PR (Personal Record) that day and you did so by 4 seconds. Whatever happened to you that day, whatever came over you that day, you displayed the HEART of a CHAMPION because you COMPETED. For the first time in your track career, you broke 60 seconds in the 400m. That day, you were timed at 56.5. That day you COMPETED. Your team did not make it to the finals, but you did COMPETE. The younger, diminutive guy ran faster than the older, larger guys on the team. The younger, slighter guy ran with HEART. The younger, smaller guy COMPETED!

At this year's Amateur Athletic Union (AAU) Nationals when you took the track for the 400 m semi-finals, you knew you were a long shot to make it to the finals. You knew that your best chance to make it to the finals during the Junior Olympics (JO) was in the 800 m, an event that just days ago, you had run your slowest race of the outdoor season. In spite of every reason to pack it in, to just give up, to just go through the motions, you went out and PR'd again in the open 400m running a 58. The fact that you could not win a medal, the fact that you would not earn All-American status again did not deter you from giving the BEST EFFORT you had EVER given in the open 400m. Two consecutive days in a row, you BROUGHT it. Two consecutive days, you COMPETED when lesser men did and would have quit.

I could go on and on with examples about your history of being a FIGHTER, of finding the HEART to COMPETE, but the day is not that long and my fingers are beginning to cramp. The thing I wanted you to know is that I BELIEVE in you and I BELIEVE that when you make it up in your mind to COMPETE, there is no one better than you. Keep in mind, like I always tell you, that this thing called life is a PROCESS. The more you FOCUS on giving your MAXIMUM EFFORT, having a CAN DO ATTITUDE, and being FEARLESS, and the less you focus on the OUTCOME and what others do better than you, the MORE legendary historical moments you will experience.

Whenever you are playing soccer, whenever you are on the track, in the classroom and someday at the office of your company, you must ALWAYS, ALWAYS COMPETE. You are going to find that most of your competitors on the field, in the classroom, and in the boardroom don't know how to WORK HARD; they don't know how to COMPETE. When you COMPETE they are going to be confused, frustrated and more often than not they are going to give up. Yes, the kids with supposed "great foot-skills" (the prima donnas) are going to give up because they can't match your FOCUS, TENACITY, and DESIRE.

Tomorrow when you get on the field do not go to play soccer; NO don't go to PLAY soccer. Do not spend one millisecond worrying about making mistakes or not meeting the coach's expectations. Instead get on the field and simply COMPETE!

Control what you are able to control: your FOCUS, your EFFORT, and your ATTITUDE. If you do this, you will have competed and the OUTCOME will be obvious and exactly what you DESIRED.

Dad

Questions

1. The article that the father begins the letter quoting says kids don't know how to do what?

2. What is the difference between simply playing a game and competing?

3. Why does the father say not to worry about winning?

4. Have you ever been in a situation that you believed you couldn't win in school or in sports? What did you do?

5. Name some times that you know you "competed".

6. Did you know that you have the ability to do anything your mind can conceive?

Chapter Thirteen: Just the Two of Us

The last seven and a half hours were among the worst moments that I can remember in my life. The agony began as I walked down the dark, desolate and lonely hallway which leads from your room to the corridor where the driver was awaiting me at 4:50 this morning to take me to Guarulhos International Airport in São Paulo, Brazil. The walk felt ominous and foreboding similar to the walk John Coffee made as he was being led to his execution in the *Green Mile* (King and Darabont 1999).

Thank God, I had not been wrongly convicted and sentenced to death for the rape and murder of two white girls. Instead, like John Coffee, I had to say good bye to the world or in my case the biggest part of my world. Like John Coffee, I feared the darkness of the hallway and walk through the corridor and I cried uncontrollably (as I am now).

At 4:50 am in Porto Feliz, Brazil, I had to say my see you later(s) to you, my son, my best friend, the beat of my heart, the pulse of my soul. You see, while you are training and playing soccer abroad this school year, this will be the first time in your seventeen years on this planet that you won't be easily accessible to me. I realize that you have been away from home a number of times before but never like this. This is something altogether different, and it hurts like hell.

Everyone says you'll be okay. However, with all due respect, none of those attempting to provide me comfort have ever been in my shoes. A child living in a foreign country where he barely knows the language, leaving him in the hands of people that I can't communicate in person with let alone without a translator, living in a city where no direct flights exist to reach him... As I write this, I am growing increasingly uncertain about this decision more so than at any time previously.

Maybe I should have planned to stay with you for the first couple of weeks. The downside to that is that you might always be seen with me and thus perceived as the "unapproachable American" by the other players. My personality has always been the perfect complement to one as initially introverted as you. Without my "never meeting a stranger style", you could be there for weeks and never be any more connected to your new surroundings than the first day of arrival.

So there we were last night at about 10:30 pm preparing to say good night while we were both seemingly reluctant to do so. Neither one of us wanting to be the one to turn off the final light switch. Neither one of us wanting to be the first to get in the bed and under the covers. It felt as if simply preparing to say "good night" was an admission that the world would be altogether different tomorrow – as if we would find ourselves banished to some alternative universe where we would never be heard from again.

As you prepared your belongings for the next day, I could see the trepidation in your eyes. So I held you, my baby boy. You the young man who only moments earlier was doing his best to put on the face of confidence and fearlessness broke down. As I held you in my arms, I felt your body grow limp and I heard you begin to cry. Your sniffles turned into a painful collection of tears. You cried the likes of which I do not ever remember hearing from you before. As you cried, I cried (just as I am at this moment). I cried because I wanted so badly to help you but the help that I could offer would not serve you at all. For the first time in your life, I felt completely useless to you – neither taking you home nor would staying with you serve you in your *Pursuit of Happyness* (The Pursuit of Happyness 2006).

I know you are hurting, but outside of moving into the Academy permanently, I don't know what more to do. Again, I question the soundness of this decision, and wonder if somehow I have failed you yet again. At this moment, all that I am able to do is remind you that I love you equal to the love that any man could have for his son. I am so extremely proud of you, and yet once again you have exceeded my ability and surpassed my expectations.

I want you to know that whenever you need me, I'll be there just like the lyrics from Will Smith's song "Just the Two of Us" from the 1998 album *Big Willie Style*. As I write, tears are streaming down my face while I hum the lyrics to the song:

> *I'm always here for you,*

Look over your shoulder I'll be there;
Whatever you need just call on me,
We gonna rise we gonna shine;
Whatever you need I'll be there for you any time,
Just the two of us, you and I!

A parent never wants to see or hear the type of pain that I heard and felt last night. I keep telling myself that this is the journey you have chosen for yourself and no worthwhile journey will ever nor should it ever occur on "Easy Street" or shall it be paved in gold.

You have dared to dream of soccer greatness and all the greats have stories of triumph over tragedy, success where none seemed possible, and victory where no believers initially existed. I suppose the last now eight and a half hours are part of your journey, an important chapter in your story and what is meant by paying your dues.

Damn this hurts!

Dad

Questions

1. In this chapter, the father is saying goodbye to his son as he goes to play soccer abroad. What are the main emotions that the father is feeling?

2. Why does the father believe that it is best for his son to go abroad alone?

3. Have you ever had to say goodbye to your best friend?

4. Should the father have stayed with his son?

5. Would you be willing to live alone in another country to pursue your dreams?

6. Should the son have gone home with his father?

Chapter Fourteen: Kairos

Dear Naeem:

You are my dearest and most favorite son. Yes, I know what you are thinking – you are my only son. While your thoughts and comments are true, I could – nevertheless – feel about you in the unfortunate way that far too many parents feel about their children. In short, I could consider you my least liked and least appreciated child. Quite the contrary though, I love you man!

For the past sixteen years and nine months, I have loved you and have been consistently in awe of you. I have – by every single breath you take – been able to become a better man. From the day that your mom began yelling *"it's plus, it's plus"* (referring to the home pregnancy exam) to the time when you were two, upset about having to take a nap and said to me *"Daddy you are rude and foolish, you ought to be ashamed of yourself and you owe me an apology"*, I started to become a better man. From the time when you finished horribly at a national track meet and ran off lamenting your results, to the time you returned home and created a plan and committed to becoming a national finalist, I have been able to become a better man. Even last evening when you crumpled up my papers that were in the printer because you were *"getting frustrated"*, I continue to become a better man. Yes, believe it or not. Even in your moments of lunacy, I become a better man. Think about it. A lesser man might have put you out of the house. You are not homeless, are you?

Besides to make you homeless says as much if not more about me than it would about you. As I have always said, I am only successful when you are successful. I only progress when you progress. You are the fruit of my tree and as such when you do something honorable, I am admired. When you do something unworthy, I am shunned. We are inextricably and forever linked. We are like the sun and the rays that are emitted. We are like water and the ripples that flow. For better or for worse, Soop, we will always be Jor-El and Kal-El (Superman's biological father and Superman) (Siegel and Shuster 1938).

My beloved son, you mean the world to me and without you, I'm not sure that my life would have the meaning that it has today. You are the best parts of me. Most parenting experts frown upon my next admission but frankly who cares. We both know that I rarely do what everyone else says. You are my best friend. You are the fulfillment of everything that I could ever have imagined having a son and being a father would be. I would be absolutely lost without you. Again, I love you man!

I can't believe it but your high school years are nearly concluded. I know things have not gone the way you imagined that they would have gone. I am extraordinarily sorry about that! I feel as though this is the one area of your life where I have absolutely let you down. Without question, you deserve much better than you have received the past three years.

Yet despite the difficulties and hardships that continue to be heaped upon you, you manage to resiliently rise, going about your day with grace and dignity. Your perseverance to rise each day and keep your head up is yet another example of how I am better for being in your presence. Furthermore, your ability to not only endure hardship but to progress in those less than optimal circumstances is proof that we named you appropriately.

Naeem Khari, don't ever stop behaving as the **Benevolent King** that you were born, named and raised to become. I am humbled and honored to be your father. I am even more grateful and ecstatic to call you my best friend.

In case, I have not made it quite clear, I love you man!

Dad

Questions

1. In this chapter, the father hints at his son's disappointment, and that even with these challenges, his son persevered. How do you handle disappointing situations?

2. Is there anyone you feel inextricably linked to?

3. The father says that his son has made him a better man. How?

4. What are your thoughts about parents and children being best friends?

Chapter Fifteen: Knocking A Man Down Doesn't Make You Taller

Naeem:

Tough game today. I thought you all played a pretty good first half. However, after your teammate was hurt, it seemed as if the air went out of the team's collective sail.

Regrettably, much worse than your teammate's injury, which will undoubtedly heal, is the way the team behaved: mentally and emotionally collapsing after the game. Unfortunately, you were one of the team members that I along with others adults witnessed behaving in a less than positive fashion.

Believe me; you know me well enough to know that I know what it feels like to be frustrated and want to lash out at my opposition. In full disclosure, I have certainly been guilty a time or two in my life of letting my emotions get the best of me, which is why I feel compelled to share this thought with you: "just because you knock a man down doesn't make you taller".

What do I mean by this? In short, if a man is 6 feet tall and he is knocked to his knees, he may only be 4 feet 6 inches on his knees. Even if the man who knocked him down is 5 feet 6 inches, the 5 foot 6 inch man does not suddenly become taller. The 5 foot 6 inch man is still exactly 5 feet 6 inches. He does not get to elevate himself by adding the reduced inches from the 6 foot man to his own height.

Today, when H.D. made disparaging remarks about your abilities, you decided to knock him down so that you would feel better – so that you would be the taller man. The unattractive truth is that you did not grow one inch today: you were neither the taller, better, nor victorious man, for having responded to him in the way that you did.

I know life is challenging at times, but this is where real men step up and set themselves apart. Do not fall short where I have fallen short. Do not fall into the pits that I have fallen into. You can be a better man than me. You must be a better man than me.

You and I know that H.D.'s statement was not true. We also know that he made his unfortunate statement out of frustration, and to say the least, very poor adult influences. However, what you said and the way you said what you said, mimicking his inability to speak as succinctly as you, was a real blow that could leave an indelible mark on him. His inability to speak as succinctly as you is a truth that is not as easily corrected as simply as it will be for you to perform better the next time your team takes the field.

No matter what he said, you simply could have elected another way to respond. You could have reminded him that you all are supposed to be on the same team and attempting to belittle another is not what real teammates, less real men do. You could have simply reminded him that we as humans are all flawed and full of imperfections, and that you would give him the humane consideration that he did not afford you by not highlighting his flaws and imperfections.

In other words, you could have instead helped a man, who was unaware that he had already been knocked to his knees, stand up. Instead of helping him, you stood over him figuratively with your fist clenched, as if to say look who is the big man now. You, however, had not grown one inch. You were physically the same size as you were before you decided to engage in demeaning conversation. You, however, had shrunk figuratively because of the way you handled the situation.

Please don't receive this as a stern critique of you as a budding man. This is simply the effort of a man with great flaws trying to help his extraordinary son become the best man that his great promise and potential will allow him to be. Again, I, of all people, know what it is like when you want so desperately to put another in their place. Yet, there are times, like today, when a quiet dignity is far more expressive than a powerful punch to knock another to his knees. I am confident that in the future you will understand the appropriate time and place to be benevolently noble. After all, you are named Naeem Khari – the Benevolent King.

Love you,

Dad

Questions

1. Explain what the father means by "knocking another man to his knees".

2. How did the father want his son to handle the confrontation that he had with his teammate?

3. How would you have handled a disagreement with a teammate?

4. Why does the father remind the son that his name means Benevolent King?

5. The term "quiet dignity" refers to what type of behavior?

6. What do you believe the father meant when he refers to himself as a "man with great flaws"?

Chapter Sixteen: Love and Futbol

Hey Poot:

The other day when I was talking to you about your commitment to soccer, I wasn't sure if the pitch of my voice overshadowed the spirit and intent of my message. For that reason, I have decided to try to explain what I meant in writing.

For starters, I do not want you to think that I don't believe you when you say that you love soccer. I unquestionably believe that you believe you love soccer. Unfortunately, I have been on the planet just a tad bit longer and I have experienced everything from a school boy crush to real love. It is my time and experience on this planet which provides me with a greater understanding of what love really is. I am sorry to say that the love you express for soccer is more akin to a school boy crush or what is affectionately known as "puppy love".

In due time though, I am certain that you will understand that the love you profess for soccer today is not really love at all. Truthfully, I hope that you figure it out much sooner than later – as love waits for no one. If you don't love the game, the game will love another. The game will not wait idly by for you to figure out how to love her. The game, like a good woman, will want to be loved. The game, like a great woman, will demand that she is loved now – continuously and appropriately without exception.

In a time far, far away (I can only hope), you will actually know exactly what I am referring to – the love of a great woman. You will then understand this letter much more. You will know later that the current way that you show love to your proclaimed future vocation will only lead you to heart break if you someday love a woman the very same way. In the meantime, I will do my best to help you understand in a way one – like you – who has not known real love and real heartbreak can understand.

According to Webster's Dictionary, Love is "the object of attachment, devotion, or admiration." I think that we can look at the three words that Webster uses to define love to illustrate why and how the way that you treat soccer is less like love and more like a school boy crush, "puppy love".

The first descriptor of Love, attachment, connotes the physical connection by which one thing is attached to another. In the case of you and soccer, by this definition you and your soccer ball should be one. The two of you should be permanently connected. With rare exception should there ever be a time when anyone should see you without your ball.

One day, you will know the love of a great woman and this descriptor will make all the more sense to you. Hopefully, you will meet a woman who captivates you to such an extent that you cannot bear the mere thought of being any place other than where she is. Everything about her will constantly resonate in your mind and you will feel a painful longing to be in her presence the very moment she is away from your side. Each passing moment that you are apart will feel like a lifetime. My dear and beloved son, this is what it means to be attached.

This my son is what becoming what you hope to become as a soccer player will require. Like being away from the great woman you love, it must hurt when you are not playing the game. Like being near the woman you love, it must be pure joy each and every time you touch the ball as it will be when you touch her hand. I'm not sure how you learn to love soccer the way you will one day love a great woman, but you must discover a way to love the game in the same manner if your dream of playing at the highest level is ever going to be a reality.

The second descriptor, devotion, signifies a state of being ardently dedicated and loyal. In the case of you and soccer, by this definition you would be so passionate about all things soccer that your dedication and loyalty to the sport and it as your craft would be unmistakable. As with the love of a great woman, you will simply not want to be with anyone other than her. You will find her beauty unparalleled even when the masses consider another more beautiful.

This woman is a woman who will have won you over with her willingness to love you back in the way that you most need and desire to be loved. This woman will understand and personify what I call the Immutable Law of Reciprocity. She will nourish you properly when mind, body and soul are malnourished, she will clothe you when your clothes and spirits are torn and tattered, and she will always inspire you so that others will be unable to tear you down.

Loving soccer similarly, being dedicated and loyal, can propel you to experience success in the game. This dedication has the potential to make sure that you and all those you love never go hungry, and that you and those you love never have a concern about what to wear. Most importantly, this dedication will ensure that you and those you love will forever be overjoyed with what you have been able to accomplish.

As with the love of a great woman, you must only love soccer – devoting all your time and energy to the perfection of your talents and knowledge of the game. A great woman will desire and ask for nothing less. The pursuit of excellence in soccer makes the very same request: complete dedication and unwavering loyalty.

The third descriptor, admiration, indicates a delighted or astonished fondness. By this definition, you would be delighted each and every time you see your soccer ball: you would not waste an opportunity to juggle your ball, learn a new move, and/or do anything that would allow you to spend time with your ball.

The same will occur with a great woman. You will light up from the inside out whenever the mere thought of her crosses your mind. It will feel as if your heart and soul are smiling simultaneously. There will be a warm tingling glow that cascades over you as you anticipate her arrival. And when you are near her, it is almost indescribable how magnificent you will feel. Your words will be slurred. Your thoughts will be jumbled. Your heart will beat so fast as if it was coming out of your chest. Best of all, she will feel the exact same way that you do and she will have the same physiological experiences. Any and all in your company will know that you two are in love.

Admiring soccer must conjure up these sorts of feelings and physical reactions for you. Your heart must beat with joy each time you run through defenders with the ball. Your feet must jump with joy each time you leap to head the ball. Your entire body must tingle when you smell the freshly cut grass on the field as you anticipate what the next 90 minutes has in store for you.

This is the admiration that is required to be one of the all-time greats. This is the admiration that is required to make a mark on the game. This is the admiration that is required to make the world remember you until the end of time. Like a great love which is remembered forever, you must commit to loving the "beautiful game" the very same way.

Son trust me, when you meet that one good, great woman, you will understand that you must love her as I have described…completely. All the elements are critical and must be in harmony. You will have to be attached (heart, body, mind, and soul). You will have to be completely, unequivocally devoted and you will have to admire her like you have never admired a woman and will never admire another.

If you do anything less, you will never know real love. If you give anything less, you will one day reflect on what could have been and this above all things is something you never want to experience. Regret of what could have been is one of the worst experiences any man could ever encounter. Do everything humanly possible to avoid this tragedy.

I realize that this letter might seem a bit off the beaten path at the moment, but there will come a day and a time that this all makes perfect sense to you. For now, my dear son, just commit to the "beautiful game" in a way that you have never before committed. Forsake all other interests (comic books, music, television, etc.) for the love of the game.

For when you really love the game, the game will love you back in the most beautiful way. And when the day comes and you meet that great woman, you will be prepared to love her correctly because the "beautiful game" prepared you to do so.

On that day, all your dreams will have become a reality. Not only will you have reached the pinnacle of soccer, but you will also have a woman at your side who will love you when the game no longer loves you back. On this day, you and I will hopefully share a quiet moment as we will once again reflect on the real meaning of love and our conversation will be a great deal more pleasant than the other day.

I can't wait!

Dad

Questions

1. The father says that there is a difference between "puppy love" and real love. What are the differences?

2. Why does the father compare his son's love of soccer to the romantic love he will experience one day as an adult?

3. What are the three aspects of love that the father wants the son to understand?

4. The father says that devotion is a requirement of love. Do you agree?

5. How would you describe love to someone who had never known romantic love?

6. Do you think the son ever expressed love for soccer the way the father implored him to do?

Chapter Seventeen: No One Believed

Naeem:

The links below pay tribute to all those teams and individuals that no one believed were good enough. Every one of those teams and individuals shared similar qualities:

1. They believed they could win. They believed they were good enough. No matter what anyone else thought, they recognized that they put their pants on just like their competitors, they wore a jock strap just like their competitors, their blood was the same color as their competitors, etc. So if everything was the same as their competitors, they asked themselves a valuable question; *"why can't we (I) believe in ourselves (myself) the same way my competitor believes in themselves?"*

2. They were fearless. If no one expected them to do anything, they had nothing to fear. Only good things could happen. If they lost everyone would say things went as planned, but if they won they would change history.

3. They competed as if there was no tomorrow. They realized they had one moment to be great, and that moment was right in front of them. They did not think about yesterday (game,

practice, etc.). They did not think about tomorrow (game, practice, etc.) Instead they simply embraced the moment, and gave it all they could give.

4. They showed immeasurable guts. They gave every ounce of blood, sweat, and tears. They did not watch the clock, they did not worry about the opponents, nor did they give any focus to the spectators. Rather, they simply committed themselves to making sure that when the final whistle blew, when the game was over, they had no regrets about their performance, as they knew they had given everything they had to give on that day. They realized that worse than losing was having to look themselves in the mirror and know that they did not give it all they had to give. For them having guts meant being willing to die for the success they desired.

5. They measured success differently than the opponent. Success was making sure the opponent would never forget – win or lose – that they just competed against someone with the heart of a lion, and someone who would die before they would quit, give up, or fail to give it their all...100% and nothing less!

6. They had fun. With nothing to lose, with no one expecting them to win, much less provide any real competition, they were able to stay loose, relaxed, and simply focus on having fun. It's sports...sports are games... games that are originally and

routinely played by children…children find games to be fun…shouldn't all those who are fortunate enough and talented enough to compete in these games find joy and have fun playing?

When the whistle blew, when the game was over, after doing the things above, something surprising happened to all those below…they did something nobody believed possible…they left their mark on the world.

What about you?

Check out the links:

1. Cassius Clay vs. Sonny Liston[1]
2. Jesse Owens 1936 Olympics Adolf Hitler[2]
3. Roger Bannister Breaks The Four Minute Mile[3]
4. Joe Louis & Max Schmeling Weigh In 1938/06/22[4]
5. Young Woman and the Sea by Glenn Stout (long version)[5]
6. 1983 NCAA Basketball Championship[6]
7. Flutie's Miracle in Miami[7]
8. James Buster Douglas Knocks Out Mike Tyson[8]

---

[1] "Cassius Clay vs. Sonny Liston" [February 17, 2008], video clip, accessed February 17, 2008, YouTube, http://youtu.be/LNdmySLkqyI

[2] "Jesse Owens 1936 Olympics Adolf Hitler" [Jan 30, 2008], video clip, accessed Jan 30, 2008, YouTube, http://youtu.be/XXIe5GbLSUs

[3] "Roger Bannister Breaks The Four Minute Mile" [May 31, 2007], video clip, accessed May 31, 2007, YouTube, http://youtu.be/uz3ZLpCmKCM

[4] "Joe Louis & Max Schmeling Weigh In 1938/06/22" [September 12, 2006], video clip, accessed September 12, 2006, YouTube, http://youtu.be/7TY28c-1vyQ

[5] "Young Woman and the Sea by Glenn Stout (long version)" [June 11, 2009], video clip, accessed June 11, 2009, YouTube, http://youtu.be/IvXNhVGhfYQ

[6] "1983 NCAA Basketball Championship" [March 26, 2008], video clip, accessed March 26, 2008, YouTube, http://youtu.be/8l5N2eKdvL4

[7] "Flutie's Miracle in Miami" [November 17, 2006], video clip, accessed November 17, 2006, YouTube, http://youtu.be/q3ykWbu2Gl0

9. Newscast from 1991 Duke beats UNLV[9]

[8] "James Buster Douglas knocks out Mike Tyson" [March 17, 2009], video clip, accessed March 17, 2009, YouTube, http://youtu.be/rt8LZ8FjGN8
[9] "Newscast from 1991 Duke beats UNLV" [May 6, 2007], video clip, accessed May 6, 2007, YouTube, http://youtu.be/okNOOcPmnZM

<u>Questions</u>

1. What do you think is the most important characteristic for a person that wants to leave their mark on the world? Why?

2. What were the shared qualities of all the people and teams the father writes about?

3. Why does the father want his son to remember that most sports originate as games played by children?

4. How does the father believe success should be measured?

Chapter Eighteen: Nothing to Fear but Fear Itself

Dear Naeem:

I have to admit that earlier when you mentioned being scared, I was caught off guard. I didn't say anything immediately because I did not want to seem insensitive by replying in some macho, off the cuff, little introspective fashion. I hope you know that responding in the aforementioned way is just not my style. Instead, I chose to simply give you my full undivided attention and listen attentively to what you had to say.

Believe it or not, there are times when even I believe being silent and just listening is the best, most appropriate thing that I can do for you as your father. I learned this lesson from your great grandmother as she use to say that God gave us two ears and one mouth for a reason. I'm fairly certain that she would be glad to know that every now and then that I can still listen to her, and even God for that matter. I imagine that if she could, she would probably say to me, "Thank God that you have two ears".

In hindsight, while I followed my grandmother's instructions by not letting my mouth overshadow my two ears, I think I might have failed you. Even though I am convinced that you did not want me to respond with some chauvinistic nonsense, I now sense that you wanted me to say something that could ease your fears. So let me begin by apologizing for not giving you what you needed at that moment. Hopefully, you'll allow me the opportunity to make it up to you, and you will find something both comforting and useful in the words that follow.

Son, I am no different – no exception – no stronger than you. In fact, like you, I have often found myself fearful of people, places and things. My life experience has left me convinced that the thing that has often scared me more than any person, any place or anything has been the fear of the unknown. For as long as I can remember, the uncertainty about a future event caused me more angst than anything else. The uncertainty about an event that I had no assurances would come to fruition – because as your great-grandmother would say "tomorrow is not promised" – left me unduly shaking and quaking in my Timberland boots.

I can even remember when your grandmother (after I did something that I wasn't supposed to do) would say to me "wait until your father gets home". Those six words, "wait until your father gets home", caused me to shed an incalculable amount of tears and sweat infinite bullets. There were times when the fear of what was going to happen was well deserved, but there were also times when the fear was unjustified.

As I think back to those days now, the fear I had as I "waited until my father got home" was never justified; it was always unfounded. Think about it. If I was going to be punished by my father, what was the value in punishing myself before he punished me? That's two punishments for the price of one. Boy, was that dumb of me.

On a rare occasion, my father would not even punish me. However, I had already worked myself into a torrential sweat and had cried puddles. What was the value of punishing myself when he wasn't going to punish me at all? A self-imposed punishment for nothing. This was worse than two punishments for the price of one. Another not so bright move on my part.

While the words "wait until your father gets home" strike absolutely no fear in me today, those words do remind me of what we do to ourselves when we focus on what could and might happen, instead of what is happening. The thought of the fear of the unknown having such power over us also reminds me of the first inaugural address of President Franklin D. Roosevelt in 1933. During that address FDR gave the famous "there is nothing to fear but fear itself" speech. In his address he said:

> "So, first of all, let me assert my firm belief that the only thing we have to fear... is fear itself — nameless, unreasoning, unjustified terror which paralyzes needed efforts to convert retreat into advance." (Roosevelt 1933)

While FDR was not talking about the things that scare you or me specifically when he gave the address, he was precisely accurate. The only thing we have to fear is fear itself. Fear of the unknown. Fear of something that is nameless. Fear of something without reason. Fear that is just plain old unjustified.

This is precisely the fear that I experienced when your grandmother uttered those six words "wait until your father gets home". My father wasn't home and instead of enjoying the present moment, I was fearing what might happen…what if my father happened to come home…what if he came home before I went to bed…what if your grandmother even planned to tell him how I had misbehaved…what if the whipping would hurt…

What if, what if what if… What a waste of time and energy considering all the "what ifs" that existed! There I was, paralyzed by the fear of what might or might not, what could or could not happen. There I was, retreating to some self-imposed punishment, when I could have chosen the opposite of fear: to be calm and composed, especially given that there was nothing harmful occurring to me at that moment.

I wasn't getting a whipping. There was no cussing or screaming directed towards me. Yet, I was so fearful about the fear of the unknown that I didn't see the glass as it really was: half full. I could have gone outside and played with my friends. I could have enjoyed my toys. I could have done any number of fun things, particularly if "when my father got home" I was going to be on some lengthy punishment, where I was forbidden from interacting with my friends or playing with my toys. Yet, there I was, withdrawing to my room, lying in my bed, shaking and convulsing uncontrollably, and crying my eyes out for nothing.

What I should have said to you earlier was, please son, do yourself an enormous favor: don't live your life this way. This is exactly what I should have said to you earlier, and I apologize again for not having done so. When faced with the unknown, see the glass as being half full: full of promise, possibility and potential.

Don't spend your time being fearful about something that may never happen, and if it does by some rare chance occur, it will almost always be worse in your imagination than it will ever be in reality. Enjoy your life to its fullest. Don't stop playing with your toys and friends, literally or figuratively, out of some unjustified fear.

Trust me, I received a number of whippings from my father, and none of them were as bad as I imagined them to be as when I let fear get the best of me. Don't let the fear of the unknown paralyze you and keep you from taking advantage of, and participating fully in, the opportunities life places before you.

You only get one life to live, and I can assure you that you don't want to spend your one life living in fear. Take the words of FDR and turn them on their axis. Repeat these words whenever you sense fear attempting to creep in, "I have absolutely nothing to fear; this moment is full of promise, potential and possibility."

My most sincere apologies,

Dad

P.S. If you really want to kick fear in the butt, give a name to the things that are promising – full of potential and possibility – in your life. Think positive. And remember the glass is never empty, it is always some percentage of full.

Questions

1. Why does the father say that fear of the unknown is unnecessary?

2. Why is worrying about what may or may not happen a waste of time, according to the father?

3. Who is FDR?

4. The father wants the son to believe the glass is never empty. Why does he want his son to view life this way?

5. What are the words that the grandmother used that made the father fearful?

6. What are some situations that make you fearful?

Chapter Nineteen: One Word That Can Destroy Everything You Hope to Achieve

---

Dear Naeem:

I want you to read the following quote and commit it to memory:

> "Excuses are the tools of the incompetent - Used to build monuments of nothingness - Those who use excuses are seldom good for anything else." (Unknown n.d.)

Now that you have read the quote once, how about you read this quote aloud, oh let's say another 200 times.

Okay, I'm joking, I'm joking. Maybe not 200 more times, but seriously commit this poem to memory ASAP.

A LONG, LONG TIME AGO IN A GALAXY FAR, FAR AWAY

Twenty plus years ago (and yes I know I am getting older – I don't need a reminder from you) I was forced to learn this poem. Learning the poem was a prerequisite of membership into my fraternity. When the Fraternity introduced this poem to me, I thought to myself "I have to learn another stupid poem to recite to a bunch of immature men". (I suspect you might be feeling the same way as I ask you to learn this poem, if so keep your thoughts to yourself because you are going to learn this poem whether you like it or not.) Just between you and me, the real impetus for learning this poem was to keep from going to jail.

One of my fraternity brothers was such a complete %#@&*. He bugged me about that poem every time that I saw him. All I really wanted to do was punch him, as is often the case with testosterone heavy, but short on maturity young men.

Fortunately, my line brothers convinced me that learning the poem was preferable to spending time reciting love letters to someone named Big Bubby in prison, so I learned the poem. In a cruel ironic twist, learning the poem had no appreciable effect on the kind of @#$%&* that my fraternity brother turned out to be, but the poem has been of immeasurable value to me over the years. As such, I wanted to share this poem with you as early in your life as possible.

WHOSE LIFE IS THIS ANYWAY?

There have been times when I have found the poem to be an inspirational reminder of how life should be approached. I believe it will help you focus so that you may expedite your dreams and desires much more efficiently and expeditiously than you would have ever thought possible. I believe as you digest the words and absorb the significance of this poem, you will appreciate its great truth and find yourself motivated beyond your current level.

Since learning this poem, I have found the words are unquestionably true. Not only do excuses keep us incompetent, but excuses also make us weak. The propensity to find a reason – come up with an excuse – for why we cannot do something leaves us living a life not with monuments of effort, accomplishments and greatness, but instead leaves us living a life filled with monuments of NOTHINGNESS that display all our *wish I would haves, should haves, and could haves* for all the world to see.

The predisposition to undermine our own potential that is described in the poem when we look for, make up and create excuses keeps people from knowing just how exciting life can and is supposed to be. Instead of living life in its fullness and fullest possibility, people end up living a life that never quite seems like it is the life they should be living.

A DISEASE OF EPIDEMIC PROPORTION

Excuses are a disease and even I, at times, have been an unwitting carrier of the insidious disease. More than I care to admit, I have found myself uttering the words that all those who have been infected utter, "this is not my life or at least not the life I am supposed to be living."

Curiously, I'm not certain if I am responsible for the infection of others, or if others are responsible for my infection, but somehow, far too many people have been infected with this most insidious disease. There are even a few other people in your life that have been infected with this disease. Unfortunately, they continue to be clueless about realizing that they are walking around with this deadly disease, and are potentially infecting any and all with whom they come in contact.

IN THE WORDS OF JESSE JACKSON "KEEP HOPE ALIVE" (J. Jackson 1988)

While I realize all this talk about a diabolical disease is discouraging, I don't want you to lose hope. There is some good news. The good news is that there is a cure. There are those whom you look up to and seek counsel from who have taken the first step to recovery – admitting that they have been infected. For those who have yet to be clued in on their current state of being, you would only need to ask them one question, and their response would tell you that they need and should get help.

TIME TO PLAY DOCTOR

In fact, I think you should take it upon yourself to conduct a one question poll of all those who make up the "Village of Naeem". Ask them the following: "When you think back to your childhood, is this the same life you dreamt or imagined living?" Wait for it, wait for it; don't rush the response, be very silent and patient! The answer will come after they look awkwardly in the sky with a slight squint of the eye, their foreheads will begin to get a wrinkle or two, and then they will take a deep sigh and start frowning to one side of their mouth. I'm convinced that the overwhelming majority will open their mouths and say one of the following three statements:

1. The life that I am currently living is nothing like the one I imagined;

2. I simply never took the time to dream about my future; and/or

3. My current life often feels like I am having an outer body experience – watching someone else live my life in a most undesirable and unintended fashion!

After the masses provide you with one of the three aforementioned responses and I say "I told you so", you should ask yourself the very important question: how did the people that I love and have the most respect for end up living without dreams and imagination? How then does the multitude end up infected with the diabolical and insidious disease of excuses?

A WORD FROM OUR SPONSORS: THE EVIL TWINS

As is my customary role, I will give you a clue so that you don't waste precious non-guaranteed time searching for the answer. The answer can be found in just two words, our evil twins: justification and rationalization.

We – a word which embarrassingly and unfortunately includes me – find a way to justify and rationalize just about anything and everything. We justify why we haven't done A-B-C. We rationalize why we can't do X-Y-Z. All of our justifications and rationalizations doom us to living an undesired and unintended life. All these excuses leave us to live a life made up of mostly scraps; bits, crumbs, small pieces, if you will, of what we could have, should have and would have been.

I'm sure you knew this already, but scraps, bits and crumbs of anything ordinarily are not very filling or satisfying. Most people hate leftovers. It should go without saying then that living a remnant of the life you could have, should have and would have lived is akin to not living at all. The aforementioned life is the most pathetic existence.

IT COULD HAPPEN TO YOU

From the poem, you should glean that it is crucial for you to be very particular about those whom you spend time with, otherwise you too could easily and unknowingly become infected, subjecting yourself to a pathetic existence. Even when you spend time with those in your "Village", pay particular attention to how they address each moment of their life. Your observations will show you a few things:

- How they became an easy host for the insidious disease;
- The procedure to cure you of the disease should you ever become infected; and

- The preventive treatment that will keep you from ever becoming infected.

AN EQUAL OPPORTUNITY OFFENDER

As you analyze and evaluate the members of your "Village" you will find that this disease does not discriminate based on race, color, gender, religious beliefs, national origin, disability, genetic information, pregnancy, veteran status, sexual orientation, or any other issue that the U.S.A. finds to be a problem that can only be resolved through the passing of laws. This is a disease that affects and infects any and all. You will even discover that this disease even invades the lives of those whom we hold in the highest esteem.

Again, your "Village" is proof of the universal outbreak status and potential of the disease. Despite even all the cumulative years of education, vast life experience and overwhelming number of degrees amassed, you will find that the infection of those in your "Village" occurred just the way they do for everyone. No, they did not have some absurd mythological interaction with an African Green Monkey. (Ankomah n.d.) No, they did not get it from a viral epidemic that originated when someone coughed on them on a plane. No, it was not transmitted from a virus detected in a hog slaughter house. You watch way too much television.

Everyone you know, each and every one of us, gets the disease the same old fashioned way: we earn it. Those infected have it because we lived and continue to live life in a "sooner or later" fashion. Rather than living life healthy and uninfected – living life the only way it was intended and should be lived in an exciting "here and now" manner – most of those in your "Village" live life as if there was some outright assurance that tomorrow's opportunities for life are better than the opportunities provided by the present moment.

TOMORROW IS NOT PROMISED

The fascination humanity as a whole has with what could, may and might happen tomorrow is absurdly and patently contradictory to the way life was designed for us to experience it. This may be because most people have forgotten, or worse, did not know, that life has an undetermined and yet guaranteed expiration date. Perhaps, we all need to be reminded of a few things: that if you are breathing you are getting old; when you get older you do so quickly; getting old is a stage of death; you are going to die; and today could in fact be your very last day on this earth! And if by chance, this is indeed our last day, shouldn't we all be excited about what we have accomplished and what we are doing at this very moment, rather than behaving as the infected: hoping for a do over, another day, another chance to get it right?

You would be wise with each day and each breath that you take to stay mindful of this: life and live are action words which will keep you from getting infected. I also hope that it is crystal clear by now as well that excuses are words of inaction. Excuses keep us from doing and realizing any of the things we dreamt and are capable of doing. Excuses make us take for granted each second, minute and hour that we are bestowed. Excuses make us miss out on life.

So son, if today was your last day, would you be satisfied with what you had accomplished or how you had made use of your time on this earth? Or would you instead be among those who find comfort in the standard excuses that derail their potential? Such as:

I was so busy at work or school

I had to work late

I had to study

I'm too tired

I've tried this sort of thing before but it has never worked

I don't know how to change

I have so much going on

I'm scared

I'm not that smart

I'm not special

I can't do that

I don't want people to know my fears

My dog ate my homework

I didn't have enough time

I'm too old to change my life now

This is good stuff for young people

Blah, blah, blah, blah…blah

Learn the poem! If you learn and live the poem, I believe your answers will always be that you are satisfied with what you have accomplished and how you have made use of your time on the planet. You now have a head start on how to get rid of the willingness and ease of which the majority of the world uses excuses. Never build monuments to nothingness, as there are far too many useless shrines that exist already. Never be considered incompetent, as there are far too many unproductive people currently.

Tomorrow is not promised, so give everything you have to right now – no excuses.

Love,

Dad

Questions

1. In this chapter, the father demands that the son learn a quote about excuses. What is the quote, and what does it mean to you?

2. What is the harm in making excuses?

3. How does the father characterize excuses?

4. What excuses are you fond of making?

5. Are you living for the moment or are you waiting to start living?

6. If today was your last day on earth, would you be satisfied with what you had accomplished or how you had made use of your life?

Chapter Twenty: Process, Process, Process...Get the Vision

Naeem:

First things first, you must stay mindful that this pursuit of soccer greatness is a PROCESS. Instead of thinking of each training session as an individual practice to be measured as only pass or fail; you should instead think of your pursuit of soccer greatness as nothing more than one long practice session combined with 10,000 or more hours of deliberate effort to refine your skills and ability. You are simply not going to reach your fullest potential without having bumps and bruises, falls and failures. REMEMBER: WHAT YOU ARE TODAY IS NOT WHAT YOU WILL BE TOMORROW! What you must embrace is that each time you fall, you are falling closer to your goal. Each time you fail, you are failing closer to GREATNESS.

How, you ask, does falling and failure help? Simple, when you were a child and you were learning to walk you fell lots of times. Each time you fell, you had to figure out how not to fall the next time. You had to figure out the right way to place your feet, the right way to balance your body, the right pace to move and more. Before long, you figured out how to do those things and were able to walk without falling. Your next PROCESS was to learn to run which required the same type of deliberate practice as walking. Soccer is the same; life is the same. The difference is you.

When you were a child you approached your goals of walking and running with a childlike single focus and deliberation. If you really want to be great in soccer, you must do the same thing. Single focus and deliberation does not mean being overly critical, becoming negative and feeling despair. Rather, single focus and deliberation means that you practice with joy and calmness because you understand that you are getting closer and closer to realizing your ULTIMATE GOAL.

Single focus and deliberation means that you observe and evaluate what worked and what didn't work each and every day, with each and every practice/game. This will expedite the process of realizing your ULTIMATE GOAL.

So put all that technology that you have to good use. Evaluate/assess what you do each training that keeps you from "walking without falling". In other words, you need to record (write it down as soon as training/deliberate practice is complete) the things that are keeping you from WALKING/RUNNING in this game we call soccer.

When you record your flaws, you take the power and sting away from them and make them a documented target for improvement and measurable issues on a schedule for elimination. Equally important is recording your successes. You must record your successes, you must be balanced.

Training Suggestion for Today - Soccer Vision

Great players think a minimum of three moves ahead and do so instantaneously:

Great players anticipate the space where a teammate can move so that a good/simple pass can be made well before the teammate moves;

Great players decide where they are going to go with the ball even before it is passed to them (dribble forward attacking the midfield in 1 v1 or pass to the appropriate teammate);

If there is no pressure on you when you receive the ball, push forward...ATTACK, ATTACK, ATTACK (know where you are going and what move you are going to use to get by the opponent);

If there is light pressure on you when you receive the ball, look for the ability to make a pass to one of your forwards;
If there is light pressure on you when you receive the ball and the forwards are covered, look for the ability to pass the ball to one of your midfielders;

If all offensive options (moving to offensive 1/3) are exhausted, then and only then do you consider passing the ball back to the goalie/center back.

Great players decide IMMEDIATELY where the space is that they should move to in order to be in a position to support the player who they just passed the ball to (usually requires that the passing player must move, even if the movement is only 2 to 4 steps from where they were when they passed the ball.).

Questions

1. Why does the father emphasize to his son that his life is going to be full challenging experiences?

2. Why does the father say that it's important to document your failures and your successes?

3. Although the letter references soccer, why is vision important in life?

4. How is the story about the child learning to walk and run significant?

Chapter Twenty-One: Race Day Preparation

Good morning Soop!

There is nothing to this day. No stressing required. No anxiety needed. The world will still continue no matter what happens today. Your mom and I will love you just as we did before the meet. God will still find favor with you. With that said you should know mentally, spiritually, emotionally, and physically that you are prepared.

Say it out loud ten times, "I AM PREPARED". Yes, you are prepared. You are physically fit. You are mentally tough. Just go out and have fun today. Make the best of the day. Don't waste the day. You have been preparing well, so make use of all your preparation.

Go ahead and PR (Personal Record) today; it is okay to PR; just in case you were wondering if I would approve.

Today is just like any other day; just like practice. Go through the mental reps 3 to 5 times, i.e. YouTube videos. Visualize both races in your head over and over and over again. See yourself running the 800m with splits of no less than: 64 and 2:10. See yourself running the 200m at: 25.5 or better.

In the morning, sit up in bed, close your eyes and practice visualization:

- *See yourself winning the 800 m race.*
- *See yourself running the first 100m fast (7s per 50 or 14 per 100.)*
- *See yourself drafting off the lead runner.*
- *See yourself staying on the inside of lane one, close enough that no one can pass you on the inside.*
- *See yourself running the first 400 m at 64 pace (8s per 50 or 16 per 100).*
- *See yourself continuing to run and run relaxed at the same 8s per 50 pace.*
- *See yourself lifting your arms at your shoulders like hinges on a door (Michael Johnson/Jeremy Warner style).*
- *See your arms remaining tight on the inside.*
- *See your hands remain straight (no limp wrist curving towards your back).*
- *See yourself crossing the finish line at 2:10 or faster.*
- *See yourself winning the 200 m race from each of the lanes one through eight.*
- *See yourself run every step of the race.*
- *See yourself have a perfect start (getting out fast, low, and maximizing your first ten steps).*
- *See yourself running the first 50m or more with the IN and OUT breathing technique.*
- *See yourself run the first 100 meters fast.*

- *See yourself lifting your arms at your shoulders like hinges on a door (Michael Johnson/Jeremy Warner style).*
- *See your arms remaining tight on the inside.*
- *See your hands remain straight (no limp wrist curving towards your back).*
- *See yourself run the second 100 meters faster than the first 100m and relaxed with the longest stride possible.*

Replay this in your mind over and over again at least fifty times.

Don't just visualize the race; begin from when I would leave the room and take the elevator.

Do it when you get in the car.

Do it at the track during warm-ups.

Do it when you are called to the track.

Do it when you perform a burnout.

Do it when you do your tuck and rocket jumps.

Do it when you are getting in the blocks.

Stay focused and do not be diverted by anything.

When you get on the track:

Don't let your competitors look you in the eyes.

Don't look at your competitors.

In avoiding eye contact, you provide your opponents no information about your mental or emotional state.

In avoiding eye contact, you make your opponent worried, concerned about your ability.

Again, don't look and don't let them look. Give away no information.

Let your opponents languish from a lack of information.

Uncertainty is always disturbing. Those who are more disturbed are those who make more mistakes.

Write each quote of the following quotes in your track notebook no less than 10 times and repeat them in the mirror no less than 10 times:

"I'm prepared, God is with me so I might as well PR."

"It's just another day at the office; I mean business."

"I am Amazing, I am Supaman!"

Remember God is on your side. HE will do his part; all you have to do is do yours. Are you ready and willing to do your part? If you are ready, HE is ready! If you focus and listen, you will feel HIM run the race with you. When and if you feel weary, HE will be strong and you will feel an extra boost of power and strength!

You are ready! Go have FUN!!!!!!!!!!!!!!!!!

Questions

1. Why does the father state that the son should practice visualizing the race?

2. Why does the father encourage the son to say the same things over and over?

3. What is the purpose for writing things in the "track notebook"?

4. Why is it important to believe that you can accomplish something before you do it?

Chapter Twenty-Two: Something to Think Long and Hard About

Naeem, my son, my friend, the air that I need to live and breathe:

I have watched how you have handled the last few weeks and months of your life with keen interest. I have been interested in how well you handle the adversities of life. On some level, I am proud of your intestinal fortitude but on many an occasion I have been greatly disappointed.

You possess an unlimited wealth of gifts and talents both physical and intellectual. However, the gift that will most allow you to have the success you desire is the gift of mental toughness.

You have a modest amount of mental toughness, but you do not possess nor do you seem interested in developing the amount necessary that will make all your dreams and desires come true. You don't seem desirous of developing the amount that will allow you to benefit from the vast amounts of physical and intellectual gifts that you possess.

Life does not always give you what you want. People don't always treat you fairly or the way you deserve. In fact, you yourself don't always treat those who do the most for you the way you want to be treated. Perhaps your recent experiences are a bit of karma.

According to Buddhism, this inequality is due not only to heredity, environment, "nature and nurture", but also to Karma. In other words, it is the result of our own past actions and our own present doings. We ourselves are responsible for our own happiness and misery. We create our own Heaven. We create our own Hell. We are the architects of our own fate (BDEA/BuddhaNet n.d.).

Maybe your fortune or luck will not change until you at a minimum start treating those who do the most for you the way that you want to be treated. Perhaps then your efforts with outside, sometimes biased and ignorant people, will be more to your liking.

What little difficulties you face today are nothing compared to your ancestors. Perhaps, you need to spend less time reading comic books and watching worthless sitcoms, and spend more time reading about people who looked like you who overcame far greater situations than not playing on the "red" team.

While I acknowledge that not playing on the red team is an injustice, it is not something you cannot overcome by showing a mental toughness that allows you to be great in spite of unpleasant circumstances. A real man is one who can rise to the occasion despite difficult challenges.

The question for you now as you enter puberty and manhood is throughout your life what kind of man will you be? REAL or FAKE? STRONG or WEAK? COMPLIANT or CONFRONTATIONAL? The choices that YOU make will determine YOUR life!!!

In 1936, eighteen Black athletes represented the United States in the Olympics (American-Israeli Cooperative Enterprise n.d.). These Black Athletes and Olympic medalist faced continuing social and economic discrimination while in Germany. But when they returned to the United States they were treated with an even greater degree of racism. They were still unemployed, spat on, hated, called nigger, etc. (United States Holocaust Memorial Museum n.d.). What would you have done? Quit the team and not gone to Germany? Quit the team and not achieved the success that your talents and gifts prepared you to achieve

In the 1960s, a man named Jim Brown, the star running back for the Cleveland Browns, spoke out against the bias of the franchise owners and coaches. His outspokenness led the NFL to eventually give more black players a chance to play in the NFL.

Today, many young black men like you are so easy to forget the sacrifices like those of Jim Brown. You all refuse to speak out against any injustices, instead choosing to cower under the premise of words like "it doesn't matter" or "it won't change anything".

Thank God Jim Brown didn't think like you, or there might be the same minimal presence of African Americans in a league that is now more than 70% Black (Lapine 2009). If being treated as a man, if being treated fairly are not good enough causes to stand up for, then what will you stand up for? It has been said that a man who will stand for nothing will fall for anything. What my son do you stand for? What is worthy of you standing up for?

In the 1930s, Malcolm X watched his father die because he refused to be recognized by anything other than the man that he was (Haley and X 1965). Malcom's father was willing to die for the right to be recognized as a complete human being. You instead will let others call you names like "Spongy" in recognition of the coarseness of your hair but will not speak out against it. Yet you are never short giving unsolicited commentary when it comes to communicating with your parents.

You will not report these racists' acts to teachers, counselors, headmasters, and will even try to hide them from your parents. This is self-hate! This is the action of a coward!
God created you and your coarse hair. It serves as a protection against the elements, i.e. the sun. Instead of befriending people who disrespect you in such a fashion, perhaps you should learn to love yourself enough to tell them that your name is Naeem Khari Turner-Bandele (He who is a benevolent king despite being born from slavery and being born away from home) and not Spongy.

Although you are not Jewish, your bar mitzvah, or coming of age, is upon you. You will soon be 13; a teen, a man, no longer a boy. Your rites of passage into manhood will soon be here. Will you be prepared, or will you want the respect of a man while behaving like a boy?

Boys have to be reminded to do things; men take it on their own to see that things are done. Boys are afraid to say when things are incorrect, men speak out against injustice because they know what is done to others could very easily be done to them. Boys quit when things get tough, men work harder the tougher things get.

There are some quotes below that might assist you in your journey. Good luck manhood is knocking at your door.

I love you as your father, your friend, your mentor and as a fellow man!

- *"It's better to be prepared for an opportunity and not have one than to have an opportunity and not be prepared."* (Young n.d.)
- *"Tricks and treachery are the practice of fools, that don't have brains enough to be honest."* (Franklin n.d.)
- *"Diligence is the mother of good luck."* (Franklin n.d.)
- *"I have met the enemy, and it is the eyes of other people."* (Franklin n.d.)

Questions

1. In this chapter, the father is upset with his son because he is not speaking out about injustice. Have you ever sat back and watched something happen, either to you or to a friend, and not said anything?

2. According to the father, becoming a man is not just about getting older. What are the characteristics of being a man?

3. Who are some other people from history that you can use as examples of overcoming hardship?

4. Do you believe in Karma?

Chapter Twenty-Three: The Story of Goldilocks and the Power of Pressure

Hey My Favorite Son:

It was great seeing you and spending the last few days with you. It remains true that there is no place in the world that is better than when that place includes you. I so love you man!

I enjoyed watching you practice and play yesterday. Whenever you are on the field, you seem to be at home, even when the field you are on is 5,000 plus miles away from your actual residence. Watching your comfort on the field and in your new surroundings was reassuring; making leaving you this time a little less heart wrenching and agonizing. While you seemed comfortable on the field, there was one troublesome thing that I noticed. Something you have been guilty of most of your life – you put too much pressure on yourself.

Don't get me wrong, I know how much you want to be great. I know how much achieving your dreams means to you. However, I'm afraid the amount of pressure that you place on yourself is sometimes counterproductive. I realize that there are lots of cliché expressions about the benefits of pressure, but the truth is that pressure is not always good. Pressure can be both beneficial and detrimental.

Like most things in life there is a yin to the yang, a positive and a negative, and a blessing and a curse to pressure. Understanding this reality will be key to not only making your time away successful, but more importantly understanding the impact pressure can have will play a key role in allowing you to have the kind of life you desire.

What exactly am I trying to tell you? I'm trying to tell you that you can have pressure but the amount needs to be "just right". In fact, I liken pressure to "The Story of Goldilocks and the Three Bears" (Southey 1837). I know, I know, comparing life as a teenager to a childhood story might make us both lose some of our cool points. Don't worry about the cool points for now, though. Besides, I think my use of this story is not only going to be really useful but it is also going to be cool.

In any event, even if you don't find my analysis of the story to be cool, I know that I have accumulated enough cool points over my lifetime that I can share some of them with you if you really need them. And yes, I said it, I am the cool one and don't you forget it!

Now onto the "Story of Goldilocks and the Three Bears". To refresh your memory, Goldilocks was the little girl who went for a walk alone in the forest. Okay, one last parental deviation before I get to the heart of my message which in case you forget, is about pressure.

"The Story of Goldilocks and the Three Bears" is a children's story – yeah right! After having read this story for the first time in nearly forty years, I realize that this is a story as much about poor parenting and a substandard parenting methodology as it is about anything else. "The Story of Goldilocks and the Three Bears" is akin to a police blotter detailing the commission of one misdemeanor and felony right after the other. Moreover, the story is an example of behavior that would not have worked out as pleasantly for you and me as it does in the story.

Today, Goldilocks and her parents would be arrested by the police and ordered by the Court to receive constant supervision from the Department of Children and Family Services. Not only would Goldilocks' parents be brought up on charges of Child Endangerment for allowing a little girl to walk alone in the forest, and Child Neglect because she obviously had not been eating, but the Court might in the same way find Goldilocks' parents to be unfit and take Goldilocks away from them.

Let's also not forget that not only did Goldilocks walk alone in the forest, but she broke into the Bears' home where she ate their food, broke their furniture and slept in their beds. In the span of what was probably less than an hour, little Ms. Goldilocks should have been charged with no less than the crimes of breaking and entering, theft and conversion.

Okay, please forgive my tirade. I just had to get that off my chest. Now back to the story. For the remainder of this letter, I'm going to imagine that I am a high ranking official at Penn State University and simply pretend that I don't see any criminal behavior. Instead, I am going to share with you only the good stuff found in the story.

If you remember, after Goldilocks breaks and enters into the Bears' home, she finds three bowls of porridge. She tasted (converted) all three. The first bowl was too hot. The second bowl was too cold. The third bowl was just right. In the same way that Goldilocks (without breaking the law of course) finds a bowl of porridge to eat that is just the right temperature, you must discover the appropriate temperature, the amount of passion which is "just right". Your success now and in the future depends on you not being a hot head (too much pressure) where you appear out of control, but also not being so cool (too little pressure) that it seems like you don't care. You must find the amount of passion which is "just right," keeping you extremely engaged without losing your poise.

After Goldilocks ate the porridge, she walked to the living room so that she could sit down. My guess is that Goldilocks was a long way from home and was tired of walking, or she was barefooted and her feet were hurting from walking over the unpaved terrain of the forest. I'm just saying!

Either way Goldilocks sampled all three chairs that she found in the living room. The first chair was too big. The second chair was too big. The third chair was just right, or so she thought, until it broke into pieces. In the same way that Goldilocks (without vandalizing another's property) attempts to find a chair to sit in that is just the right size, you must discover the appropriate size of your goals and objectives – establishing expectations that are "just right".

Your success now and in the future depends on you not choosing goals and objectives that are too big for you to reach in a reasonable time frame with exceptional effort (too much pressure), but also not choosing goals and objectives that appear just right on the surface that you will shatter in no time and with minimal or reasonable effort (too little pressure). You must always set expectations for your growth, progress and development which are "just right": specific, measurable, attainable, realistic and timely.

Apparently, breaking and entering, vandalizing, and converting others property can be exhausting because Goldilocks went upstairs to take a nap. She saw three beds, and as had become her custom, she sampled all three. The first bed was too hard. The second bed was too soft. The third bed was – well wouldn't you know it – just right so she fell asleep. In the same way that Goldilocks (without behaving as an illegal squatter) finds a bed to fall asleep in that is just the right firmness and comfort, you must discover the appropriate level of self-evaluation that is "just right": fair and honest.

Your success now and in the future depends on you not being unreasonably critical (too much pressure) where you see every situation negatively as a failure or problem. But your success now and in the future depends also on you not being overly confident (too little pressure) that you appear arrogant or cocky – bragging without the requisite skills to back up your unfounded beliefs. You must find the amount of self-evaluation which will keep you hungry and determined enough to outwork everyone and self-confident enough to believe in yourself and the work you put in each and every day. Believing in yourself, putting in the work and developing the skills to back it up is "just right".

I hope you would agree that this is a very cool version of "Goldilocks and the Three Bears". If by some strange chance you don't agree that my version is not only useful but cool, perhaps I should introduce you to the *"Goldilocks, Agree with Your Parents Parenting Program"*. The program includes, but is not limited to, not feeding your child, taking their shoes and dropping your disagreeing child off at the nearest forest.

How cool is my version of the story now? I thought so!

Love ya,

Dad

Questions

1. In this chapter, the father compares putting pressure on oneself to the story of "Goldilocks and the Three Bears". When is pressure a good thing? When is it a bad thing?

2. What crimes does the father jokingly suggest Goldilocks might have committed?

3. Have you ever considered that the story of "Goldilocks and the Three Bears" was a story about bad parenting?

4. Do you have examples where you have put too much or too little pressure on yourself?

5. What are some cliché expressions about pressure that you are familiar with?

6. Do you believe the father would ever starve his son and drop him off barefooted in a forest?

Chapter Twenty-Four: Struggle Equals Progress

Hey Soop:

It has been my intention to send you this letter, ever since we trained on Monday. If you remember, when you were running those 300s (Hart n.d.) and had gotten to the point where they were difficult and painful, you lashed out at me when all I was doing was encouraging you not to quit. Oh yeah, you mumbled a bunch of things under your breath, I heard you. Not only did I hear you mumble some things, but you had the audacity to say several things that I could hear clearly. I let it slide (this time)!

It is at times like Monday, I wish there was a surveillance video that could chronicle your behavior. It would be interesting to see how you would respond to seeing for yourself just how funky your disposition can turn. It is at those times that I remember what my father's response would have been to me if I were to have reacted like you. Without a doubt, he would have only had to look at me and I would have collected myself and immediately ceased and desisted my current behavior, fearing he would knock me into tomorrow. Fortunately, for both you and I, while I am my father's son, I don't subscribe to all of his parenting methods.

Instead of yelling at you or snatching you by your collar, as my father would have done, I simply chose to ignore your outward display. I decided to let it go, as I recognized that your outward display was only a manifestation of your inward suffering that originated from your struggles to complete the 300s in the prescribed time and rest period. I decided that I was not going to let your actions instigate a reaction from me that would ruin the day, delay your training, or much worse damage our relationship.

What I watched occur to you, at that moment, was that those 300s caused you a level of discomfort, a certain amount of pain and agony, the likes of which most people ardently avoid. At that moment, those 300s were much more than training runs that would enhance your level of long speed endurance. Instead those 300s became a symbol of your tolerance for life's unforgiving discomfort, your personal threshold for pain if you will. Those 300s were at this point in your young life as close as you may have come to experiencing the hopelessness and futility that those from whom you descended endured for over 400 hundred years (The Slave Trade n.d.).

Fortunately for you, your anguish only lasted for about 50 seconds. Even more auspiciously, is that before long, the workout that caused you to struggle on Monday will have little or no effect on you in the very near future, as your mental, emotional, and physical conditioning improves. Regrettably, those whose shoulders you and I stand on today were not provided the luxury of such a brief period – 50 seconds of hardship.

In much the same way that your mind, body, and soul will adapt to the stress of the 300s, your ancestors learned to endure incomparable hardship as great soldiers. The ability of your ancestors to rise above unmatched degradation and brutality is proof yet again of the potential for the immeasurable greatness you will achieve. If your ancestors could struggle tirelessly and continuously for more than 400 years for the potential of even the slightest measure of quantifiable progress, imagine what the DNA in your body can propel you to do in the face of the battles you will encounter in life.

So there we were on the track avoiding eye contact with one another, you feeling the burn of lactic acid throughout your body and me experiencing a surprising sense of calm. We represented a sort of yin and yang; you hot and me cool. Almost as quick as you explode from your starting blocks, the following words crossed my mind:

> "If there is no struggle, there is no progress. Those who profess to favor freedom, and deprecate agitation, are men who want crops without plowing up the ground, they want rain without thunder and lightning." (Douglass 1845)

The initial thought I had when those words crossed my mind were all related to you. I thought that if you are true to your assertion that you desire success, you cannot abhor hard work; you cannot attempt to flee from difficult times, tasks, and/or duties. Instead, you must do what the vast majority of men will not; you must embrace the difficulties that are thrown at you. My second thought was that these words from Frederick Douglass were as important for me to absorb as they were for you. Those words reminded me that as your father, there will be times when nurturing you cannot, must not, and will not be easy; it will be an undeniable struggle.

Those words caused me to smile and experience the surprising sense of calm and comfort. If struggle is indeed a condition of success, how then could I be mad at you for providing a necessary element, agitation, to your own maturation? I remembered that I too was once a young man who experienced my own struggles and each of those struggles allowed me to progress to a new and higher level.

As your father, as your most immediate representation of manhood, I too must welcome and embrace lovingly the struggles that you and I share. This is indispensable, if I am to progress to become an honored and respected elder and evolve as your most trusted confidant.

As has occurred so many times in your almost 15 years on this planet, I have been inspired and enlightened by something you have done. Even when you had no intention of behaving in a manner that could be deemed valuable, your poor behavior proved to be of significant worth. Your ever so brief mental and emotional lapse triggered the contemplation of a different Frederick Douglass quote:

"It is better to build strong children than repair broken men."
(Douglass 1845)

Who would have thought something as inconsequential as having you run 300 meter repeats would have left me so encouraged about your future? Who would have thought that the events of that afternoon would have been a realization that I am on the right path to help make sure that you, my absolute and authentic legacy, continue to progress as the most brilliant and resilient man I have ever known?

As the quote infers, I must not allow you to become a broken man who needs repair. While, I can't promise you that I will always keep my cool the way I was able to do the other day; I can promise that I will make every effort to do so. I guarantee you that I will go to my grave striving to do all in my power to make sure that you are strong while you are a child so that you will be complete and unbreakable when you are a man.

Whatever we must endure to see the fulfillment of your potential and the manifestations of your destiny, bring it on! Whatever burdens we must carry to see the actualization of your visions and goals, bring them on! Whatever obligations we must meet so that you may become a sturdy and honorable man, bring them on!

Not only am I ready to meet the challenges essential to make your life synonymous with the word progress, but I welcome and embrace them!

With all my devotion,

Dad

Questions

1. Why didn't the father respond angrily when his son was upset at the track?

2. What does the following Frederick Douglass quote mean, *"If there is no struggle, there is no progress. Those who profess to favor freedom, and deprecate agitation, are men who want crops without plowing up the ground, they want rain without thunder and lightning.'*?

3. Why is the father excited about difficult moments between he and his son?

4. Is it normal for parents to embrace the challenges that arise with raising children?

5. What is meant when the father says that he and the son are like "yin and yang"?

6. The father refers to his son as *"my absolute and authentic legacy"*. What type of legacy are you creating?

Chapter Twenty-Five: Supaman's Superhero Elixir

Dear Soop,

I thought I should take a moment to tell you just how great it has been to share a couple of hours over the last several days with you. You may not understand fully the significance of the time we spend together until years from now. Fortunately, at least for me, I get the big picture right now.

Perhaps you will only grasp the significance of our time together when you are a father (something I am in no hurry to see happen). Perhaps your full recognition of the value of our time together will come once the generator which powers my existence ceases to function. Just possibly, you may already appreciate and be firmly aware of the value of our time together, and I have yet again underestimated your powers of intuition and perception. Whatever the case may be, if it takes you a few additional years to conceptualize the significance, or if you already have the full appreciation, I just want to say for the record that the time I spend with you remains as it has always been...the absolute best moments of each and every day of my life.

The last few days with you have only served to remind me that you are an exceptional person. Perhaps more importantly, you are an exceptional man. Training with you this week has allowed me to reflect on a few of the things that on the surface seem ordinary, but have been the catalyst for shaping and molding you into the remarkable person and wonderful man you are today.

Watching you this week made me think about when you, my M.I.T., first learned to run. I remember a toddler a few days shy of his first birthday on the track at Purdue running sprints with your mom and me. At the time, you could run forward but you could not stop or turn on your own. So with each sprint you ran, your mom or I would help you turn in the opposite direction so that you could return to the start and run another sprint with the next person in line. We suggested that you take a break but you were determined to run as long as we ran.

I never told you this, but I probably would have run far fewer sprints if you were not there to inspire and encourage me. How could I quit when a not yet one year old refused to quit? As I think about it now, I thought I was turning you in the right direction before you fell, but in reality it was you who was turning me in the right direction, by encouraging me to do that which would keep me healthy and extend my time on earth.

Training you this week reminded me of a four year old who ran lap after lap at North Central during the girl's high school track practice. Truth be told, I thought you were crazy.

For an entire practice you ran and ran and ran some more. Every once in a while, when it appeared that you had stopped, almost like clockwork you would reappear from behind the bushes. You were still chugging along: never missing a stride, never taking a break, resolved to run until practice concluded. Unbeknownst to you, you served as a consistent reminder to all the girls on the track team, the coaches, and parents what commitment and effort truly meant. Who on the team could complain about running intervals for 20 to 30 minutes when a four year old ran alone for the entire practice? With a role model like you, it's no surprise that the team did so well that season.

Working out with you this spring break made me remember a highly competitive pre-school through 4th grade International School of Indiana student who eagerly competed during the end of school ceremonies. You wanted not only to participate in every event, but you were determined to win every event.

By the time you were in the second grade, you were not only counting down the weeks to the end of year ceremonies, but you had mandated having training sessions so that you could assure yourself of victory. If you were going to win was never in question. The only question was how great your margin of victory would be.

Most parents assumed that your success was due to you being a child prodigy or somehow genetically blessed with gifts their children did not receive. Neither of those assumptions was correct. What those parents neglected to consider was that you were the master of preparation.

They just didn't realize that a child so young would have the interest and desire to train. Those parents didn't consider that you simply had trained much longer, much harder and with greater intentions and instruction than their children.

I hope our training the last few days has been as much a reminder to you as it has been to me that when you have the heart and spirit to prepare, you are always successful.

This week, I remembered your first USA State Track meet. You were a six year old nervous wreck. You feared the worst, as just about every kid in your events was bigger and stronger than you. You worried so much that you made me worry.

Instead of just watching young men and women run, I quickly realized how much being successful – winning – meant to you. Maybe I was at fault, given I had ordered speed suits and gold Michael Johnson sprint spikes for a six year old. (Hey: look good, do well is what I was always told) Whatever the reason, you made it clear that you wanted a gold medal that day. You finished 1st in the 400 and 2nd in the 200. Actually, I don't know if you remember this, but you were later deemed the winner of the 200 as the original 1st place finisher was disqualified because he was too old to have competed in your age division.

What I remember most from that cloudy June day was that you were successful because you had prepared at a level far greater than those who were bigger and seemingly stronger than you. (In fact, speaking of our training, there was a little regrettable experience with a tandem tow that I would like to forget about. However, it would appear that this experience was a reminder that there is no such thing as success without some bumps and bruises)

I could go on and on about all the great memories I have of watching you compete, but that was not my intention when I started this letter. What I wanted you to know is how great it is to have you as my son and my best friend.

Moreover, I wanted to remind you of something of which I hope you are always mindful. You have always been successful, not because you showed up for a meet, not because of your track outfit, nor because of your specialty shoes. You have always found success because you prepared to be successful, and when your opportunity was presented, when it really mattered, you were ready. You have always found success when you have prepared mentally, firmly visualized your goal, designed a plan of attack to achieve the goal, and were faithful and patient (yes, patient) enough throughout the implementation of that plan to see your goal achieved.

It is so very important that the 16 year old Naeem remember that the same formula that saw him run sprints before he was one year old, run lap after lap as a four year old, smash the competition at the State meet and International School of Indiana End of Year Games is the same formula that will carry him the rest of his life.

Whenever and wherever you have found success, there have been five key words that have been guiding principles, or formula if you will, for your success. Those five words have always been, and will always be "proper preparation plus patience & perseverance".

PROPER PREPARATION PLUS PATIENCE &
PERSERVERANCE! This is what enabled you to run sprints with your parents before your first birthday. This is what enabled you to visualize running with your parents, staying in your lane until someone turned you in the other direction, running until we quit. This is what enabled you to do exactly what you set out to do and more. This is what enabled you to motivate and inspire your parents to do a better job of taking care of themselves.

PROPER PREPARATION PLUS PATIENCE &
PERSERVERANCE! This is what enabled you to make it through those track practices at North Central. This is what enabled you to visualize running the entire practice without stopping, despite the heat and the loneliness of running by yourself. This is what enabled you each and every practice to do what you set out to do and more. This is what enabled you to motivate and inspire a track team that found itself at the end of the year among the State's best.

PROPER PREPARATION PLUS PATIENCE &
PERSERVERANCE! This is what enabled you to be victorious for

the International School's end of year competition. This is what enabled you to do exactly what you set out to do, as your vision of being victorious combined with your commitment to training made your victory appear effortless for all those who watched and/or competed against you.

PROPER PREPARATION PLUS PATIENCE &
PERSERVERANCE! This is not just a formula but this is YOUR formula. This is a formula that has worked from day one and it still works just as well today.

PROPER PREPARATION PLUS PATIENCE &
PERSERVERANCE! This formula will guide you to success in every future endeavor, just as it has in all previous endeavors. Remember there are no – can never be, and will never be – any short cuts. You will not have success if you have proper preparation but omit patience and perseverance. Just as you will not have success if you have proper preparation with patience but omit perseverance. No matter where you are or what you are doing, if it is in the classroom, soccer stadium, track stadium, Olympics, boardroom, Wall Street, etc., your success will always be linked to YOUR flawless undefeated formula of PROPER PREPARATION PLUS PATIENCE & PERSERVERANCE!

So as you continue to train over the coming months and years, and you find yourself faced with seemingly daunting and difficult circumstances, never forget that you have YOUR own personalized formula for success. When you put the problems or challenges up against YOUR formula, YOUR formula will lead you to success each and every time. PREPARATION PLUS PATIENCE & PERSERVERANCE is Supaman's Superhero elixir. Drink it up and see yourself succeed.

Merely Mortal,

Dad

Questions

1. In this chapter, the father details for his son a formula of success that has worked for him his entire life. Do you have a formula for success?

2. What is the "superhero elixir" that the father is speaking of in this chapter?

3. How do you define preparation?

4. What does perseverance mean to you? Give an example of a time when you persevered.

5. How old was the son when he first ran sprints with his parents? What were you doing at the same age?

6. Can you name something you have done which has motivated your parents?

Chapter Twenty-Six: Take Time to Smell the Roses

Hey Soop!

You know after our discussion last night, I thought this might be the perfect time to remind you of a couple of things. First, God has shown you immeasurable favor your entire life, and especially these last several months. You have found success in nearly everything you have ever attempted or touched – academics, social responsibility campaign, athletics, extra-curricular school activities and more. I suspect, short of listing each and every one of those accomplishments, many of them regularly go unrecognized and/or underappreciated by you.

Please, take a moment – right now – to smell the (proverbial) roses. Oprah Winfrey once said "The more you praise and celebrate your life, the more there is in life to celebrate" (Winfrey n.d.). I could not agree more. There is no better time to do so than this very moment – the only moment that matters!

Secondly, as you take a moment to praise and celebrate your life, as well as smell your "roses", also take a moment to examine the rose. When you inspect the rose, notice how each and every rose has thorns. As beautiful and as universally appreciated as is a rose, few people realize the unattractive, unappealing, and even slightly dangerous part of the rose. Few people, if any, ever take the time to notice that before the rose turns into the most recognized and beloved flower, it is only a small bud attached to a long and often extremely thick stem with particularly unattractive and prickly thorns.

Without the stem and thorns, there simply would not be a rose to admire, much less smell. Much can be said of those who achieve great and lasting success – those people who we look to as transcendent historical figures. Each and every one of these inspirational individuals had thorns that existed all throughout their lives before they became the people the world recognizes and now appreciates them for being.

The roses we all admire begin their existence in a foundation that is built on dirt and manure. The growth of the rose is further realized from a combination of regular watering, fertilizing, weeding and manicuring. Before there is any sign that the rose will bloom this is a growth-success process which is absolutely mandatory. Likewise, my dear and adored son, your growth-success process will be built on a similar course.

Your foundation will be built on your own dirt and manure: blood, toil, tears and sweat. Fortunately, there is simply no other foundation that will help you blossom in the manner that you desire and are destined. If the process was different or any less taxing, you would simply be like any other flower that will always fall short when measured against a rose. Everyone would be willing and able to do what you have done, and that which you will continue to do. If the process was altered or less challenging, you would merely be average, common, and not the transcendent figure you are destined to become. You, my iconic son, would be as ragweed growing alongside a rose – unwelcomed and quickly eliminated.

Your life has always blossomed when your foundation includes a process which has a concoction of faith and deeds combined with a blend of desire and discipline. This progression simply cannot be altered or eliminated. The only way for you to continue to smell the roses is to learn to recognize and welcome the challenges of the stem and especially those of the thorns. I don't know when additional thorns will arise, but I do know that as long as you are breathing and continue to desire and seek a life recognized for the beauty of the rose, you will continue to encounter thorns.

What is important for you to remember is that with each passing thorn you are growing ever closer to having one more moment where you can take time to smell another of your roses. Dr. Joyce Brothers said "The person interested in success has to learn to view failure as a healthy, inevitable part of the process of getting to the top" (Brothers n.d.). I believe Dr. Brothers quote infers that you cannot get to the top of the rose – the part which is honored and appreciated – without first respecting and acknowledging the growth process and the value of thorns.

I am wholeheartedly convinced that you possess a history of success to not only deal, but to succeed when those inevitable thorns arise, and that you own the methodology for growing your stem of life. Remember as your roses' blossom; take time to smell each and every one of them.

All my love, peace and happiness,

Dad

Questions

1. What are the "roses" in your life? What are the "thorns"?

2. Why is it important to "stop and smell the roses"?

3. The father says the son's foundation will be built on four elements, what are they?

4. The father quotes a few famous people, who are they?

Chapter Twenty-Seven: Thirteenth Birthday

Dear Village of Naeem:

On June 27, 2008, I will celebrate the most awe inspiring, scary, rewarding thing that has ever occurred in my life…my son, Naeem, was born thirteen years ago. Prior to his birth, I wrote a group of people whom I consider as family (both DNA related and functionally related), and asked that this group help in selecting his name. If you remember and were a part of that initial family structure, I sent ten African Centered names for males and females. The purpose of your participation was twofold: 1) I wanted to get your perspective on our decision to give him a nontraditional, non-Anglo Saxon name 2) more importantly; I wanted you to have a vested interest in his development.

I am proud to say that through the first 12 years of Naeem's life, I believe that he has lived up to his name (Naeem Khari Turner-Bandele which means He is a benevolent king despite being born from slavery and away from home). For the first twelve years, I thank you, and I am eternally gratefully. I thank you for the contributions and investments that you have made into his life, particularly those of your time and wisdom. Your willingness to share in his development and to be the "Village" that I envisioned has allowed him the ability to flourish in many areas (see attached) and begin to become the man we dreamt he would be when we first held him.

As I did nearly thirteen years ago, I am again soliciting your assistance. No, LaTonya is not expecting. You know the phrase that I am most fond of "I have my one son and I am done!" What I need from you at this point is your willingness to send Naeem something that will commemorate his first true step to manhood.

This is not a cheap request for birthday gifts or money; we are in a recession so keep your money for your own rainy days. Rather, I ask only that you send him a note, a poem, an article…anything that we could collect; a keepsake of significance that can be included in a scrapbook to commemorate the day. The aim is to provide him with a historical document that he can reference throughout his life that can serve as a reminder of all those who love him. A historical document that may provide him comfort and direction should he ever question his ability and doubt his purpose in life.

My aim is to do something similar to what the Jewish community does for Bar Mitzvah (Moss n.d.); stress that he is culpable and responsible for his actions as a member of our immediate family, as a member of our extended family (the Village), and as a member of the human family. My M.I.T. (Man in Training) should have a day that is more than cake and ice cream and gifts that will rust and turn to moth.

He should have a day where he recognizes and embraces the awesome wonder of those whose shoulders he stands on, and of those who paved the way for the life that he lives. He should also be reminded and encouraged to continue to responsibly live his life to his fullest, God-given ability.

Thank you in advance for your help! Thank you for being residents and caretakers in the village of the benevolent king!

Nate

Questions

1. Do you have a "Village"? Who (or what) does it consist of?

2. What is the meaning of the son's name?

3. Who does the father model his son's birthday celebration after?

4. What type of gift did the father want to give his son for his thirteenth birthday?

Chapter Twenty-Eight: Tomorrow

Hey Soop,

So tomorrow is another day on the journey towards the life you PLAN to live. Notice that I did not write that tomorrow is a BIG day or that tomorrow was the most important day. Instead, I defined tomorrow in precisely the terms that you should see it - as just ANOTHER day.

I also can't stress enough that no matter what happens tomorrow, tomorrow's results do not, should not, cannot and must not change your plans or deter you from doing everything in your powers to realize and fulfill YOUR life plan. Continuing to Phase III, or stopping at Phase II will have no measurable bearing on you or the journey that you have undertaken.

You would be wise to keep all these things in mind as you prepare mentally and physically for tomorrow's sessions. No matter what, tomorrow is but a blip on the radar screen. You are neither a better or worse player if you continue or stop.

You, me and most anyone with a pulse knows that the odds are not in your favor. Be it race, class, socioeconomic or other preferential measures; the deck is stacked against you. Let me be absolutely clear though, as this is not an excuse to give in, give up or feel sorry for yourself. Oh, hell no, you must NEVER do that.

Instead this is a green light to compete like a wild lion that is responsible and determined to catch his next meal for the pride. Tomorrow you fight, you exert all your heart and soul, you give maximum effort and energy to catch, defeat and devour all those who more than likely mean you no goodwill. You show them, even as they with premeditation make decisions based on factors unrelated to heart, talent, and ability, that they can NEVER EVER steal your competitive fire, dampen your belief in your ability, or dissuade you from accomplishing your life's goal.

If you don't give them hell tomorrow, they will think you are a weak and easily defeated man. If you don't give them hell tomorrow, they will think others like you can be just as easily discarded. If you don't give them hell tomorrow, they will have an easy time looking themselves in the mirror, as they justify and rationalize their prejudices and actions.

Don't you dare let them think you are weak and defeated. Don't you dare let them think others like you can be easily discarded. Don't you dare let them off the hook without having to question their beliefs and conscious.

Never forget that most of the time when you train, practice and play it is more than just training, practicing and playing. More often than not for you, you bear an unenviable burden for a weak, scared, unrighteous man. However for you this social statement – a reflection on race and class in this country – is a welcomed, easily carried burden for a man like you, "The Benevolent King". Like your ancestors before who fought so that you no longer have to ride in the back of the bus, eat at segregated lunch counters, and be treated in other inhumane ways, you have to fight the same great fight.

It seems only appropriate that as we conclude Black History Month, you have been presented with this opportunity to show your appreciation to the great brothers and sisters who fought so tirelessly for you. This is your chance as not a future leader, but a NOW leader to take the fight to them. Tomorrow for the four hours that you train, practice and play, you'll be giving your peers confidence they never knew they had to realize their dreams, and you'll be making your ancestors proud that they sacrificed everything for you.

Tomorrow make sure they never forget the name, the man, the legend that is Naeem Khari Turner-Bandele.

Questions

1. In the chapter, the father wants the son to give his opponents "hell". Why?

2. What does the father mean when he says his son is a NOW leader?

3. Why should we remember the past?

4. What is the father's intention when he tells the son that TOMORROW is just another day?

Chapter Twenty Nine: 2009 Spring Soccer Season

Naeem:

It is finally here! The first game of the 2009 Spring Soccer Season. Today you will have the opportunity to show yourself (most importantly) and all the people playing and in attendance just how committed you are to your craft. Today you will be the living vessel and physical expression of all those gifts God has bestowed on you (speed, power, agility, reaction, quickness, foot-skills, 1v1 moves, heart of a champion, and the courage of a lion).

Today you will be faster than anyone else on the field. Not only will you be faster than any other player, you will be quicker than every other player. You will be first to all 50/50 balls. Today you will be stronger than every other player. Not just physically stronger with greater endurance and muscular strength, but more importantly you will be mentally stronger.

You have stuff that the other players don't have. You have a history of people in your family who are great overcomers; folks that in spite of the odds have achieved things otherwise considered out of their reach. Your mental acumen has been challenged, and the challenge has been met in the last week or so like no other time in your athletic life. You have not let a day go by where you were not doing something that would help you as a soccer player (i.e. sprint training, medicine ball drills, juggling, foot-skills, yoga, etc.)

You are ready! You will be dominating today. People will know your name and talk about you long after the game ends. Today you will begin the first of many steps to becoming LEGENDARY.

Go out today and wreak havoc on the opposing teams. Play with the huge heart that you have and all the passion for the game that you can muster. Take on opposing players with calm, great skill and resiliency in 1 v1 and 1 v 2 situations. Demand the ball when you are matched up with a defender that you can easily beat and assist your team with a scoring opportunity. Be a leader! Be a leader! Be a leader! Show your teammates by your words and deeds how and why to give 100%.

Now wherever you are at the time you are reading this, close your eyes and practice visualization:

- See yourself with the foot-skills of Robinho who does moves that make his opponents dizzy (i.e. step-overs, sole rolls, etc.)
- See yourself with the pace of a young Ronaldo, who ran past and through all those who opposed him.
- See yourself playing with the joy of Ronaldinho who always plays with the joy of a child getting gifts on his birthday.
- See yourself with the heart of Roberto Carlos who was able to defend anyone, take the ball from them, and dribble from the

defensive half of the field all the way to his goal and score with ease.

- See yourself with the tenacity of Messi, who despite his small stature, plays like the biggest man on the field and refuses to let anyone take the ball off his foot.

- See yourself playing with the physical toughness and brute strength of Wayne Rooney who never backs down from anyone; no matter who, no matter when, no matter how.

Replay and visualize playing like those named above over and over again at least fifty times. Don't just visualize the game; actually see your face on the body of those players.

- See yourself performing step-overs with the flair and flamboyancy of Robinho.

- See yourself with the infectious smile of Ronaldinho while at the same time making no look passes with both feet and performing with dizzying creativity.

- See yourself with the incomparable foot-skills of Messi while running past other players with the ball stuck to your foot as if it was super-glued.

Stay focused and do not be diverted by anything or anyone. Remember each game you play takes you one step closer to your ultimate goal.

When you get on the field:

- Don't let your teammates' bad habits permeate your focus and knowledge about how to warm-up properly.

- Don't let your teammates' bad mental preparation and lack of focus be shared by you.

- Look at your opponents with a slight smile and twinge of confidence as if you know something that they don't know. Actually what you know is that they are about to play against a living LEGEND in the making. They are about to face SUPAMAN!

- Your belief in your talent and ability will be unsettling and disturbing to your opposition. Confidence in your own ability is always disturbing to others; often times even to your teammates. Those who are more disturbed are those who make more mistakes. Today you will play with the spirit of PERFECTION (perfect thoughts, perfect spirit, and perfect mental focus equals perfection on the field)

- Write each quote of the following quotes in your mind notebook no less than 10 times and repeat them in the mirror no less than 10 times:
    - "Do whatever it takes, win every 50/50 ball today."
    - "Be faster, be quicker than all others on the field in every aspect of the game today."
    - "I will play with a relentless pursuit of excellence, fearing not mistakes but fearing not trying everything I have trained to do and be."

Now go out and become LEGENDARY!!!!!!!!!!!!!!!!!!

Questions

1. In this chapter, the father is giving his son a "pep talk". When you have a difficult situation: a test, a game, or a performance, who do you listen to? What do you tell yourself?

2. Are you familiar with visualization? What do you visualize yourself becoming?

3. The son is encouraged to play with the spirit of Perfection. What does the father want his son to do?

4. What parts of your family history can you incorporate into your life to help you when you are having doubts about your ability?

Chapter Thirty: Visualize, Visualize, Visualize

Naeem:

It's been a long time since we have done this but it is always important to any successful athlete. SEE IT, BELIEVE IT, AND ACHIEVE IT.

Before you go out on the field today, while getting dressed, while warming up, picture in your mind everything you can about today's game. Where is the game going to take place? What is the field like? The weather? How much does your family believe in you? How much does your family love you? The more details the better – this creates stronger markers for your mind to remember and re-enact the goal you want to accomplish.

Do this whether you're scoring a goal or dribbling past a defender or making the game winning pass. Try to picture yourself making the play, and imagine how your body will move when you are faking out the opponent or taking the shot – imagine all the steps that lead up to that play. Envision ALL the things, EVERYTHING you want to accomplish.

After you have done this for a bit, let your mind take over as it will occur and you won't even realize it. Try to improve the way you picture yourself playing soccer by adding more specific details:

- Visualize where you want to play the ball and what you want to take place next.
- Visualize how well you trap the ball.
- Visualize how good your one and first touches are.
- Visualize how strong and fast you feel.
- Visualize how no one can beat you to a 50/50 ball.
- Visualize how you cannot be dispossessed of the ball.
- Visualize how well you play defense...always forcing your opponent to the out of bounds line or to support. Visualize the ease at which you are able to beat opponents 1 v 1.
- Visualize the speed at which your mind and body play the game and how you see plays two or three plays before everyone else.
- Visualize how you will not get tired.
- Visualize your ability to use every move you want and how you are able to beat your opponent.

Again, try to picture as many details as you can to make this vision as real as possible.

Remember: "Don't Cheat Yourself...Leave It All on the Field"

<u>Questions</u>

1. What does see it, believe it and achieve it mean to you?

2. Why does the father want the son to visualize the game before playing?

3. Have you ever not given your best and later wished that you could have done things differently?

4. What does the father want his son to leave on the field?

Chapter Thirty-One: When HAPPY BIRTHDAY is More Than Happy Birthday

Good morning Benevolent King:

Where and how do I begin? How about I begin with telling you how much I absolute adore and love you. Now that I have that out of the way, maybe I should begin by talking about the evils of surging and increasing levels of testosterone in a teenage male. Perhaps I should begin by talking about the tribulations of falling and diminishing levels of testosterone in 40 something men. To be honest, either hormonal related topic is somewhat depressing.

Surging and increasing levels of testosterone in teenage males do little in most cases, other than simply cause those with few life experiences and perfunctory wisdom to puff out their chest and act aggressively where neither behavior is required. Falling and diminishing levels of testosterone in 40 something men who are presumed to have significant life experiences and a profound astuteness over their teenage counterparts result in their withdrawing from relationships of any kind (marriages, children, parents, jobs, businesses, etc.) when those relationships present any undesired friction or unwarranted resistance.

The result of interactions between the testosterone supercharged teen and the testosterone challenged 40 something male are evident in many of our conversations today. In fact, the other afternoon when I asked you about whether you had called your auntie to wish her happy birthday our hormonal condition caused us to communicate in an inept and fruitless fashion. You, in the deepest baritone voice that you could muster, proceeded to tell me about your busy schedule and all the things you had to do. I, in a (who in the hell does he think he is talking to – boy let me tell you what hard work and a busy schedule really are) monotone voice, initially started to get engaged in your line of discussion but with little internal forewarning I just hung up the phone.

So before I go any further, I must acknowledge and confess that my behavior is not the type of behavior that I want to or should model for you. Thus, I offer my most sincere and heartfelt apology for not being a better role model and for letting my emotions (reduced testosterone and increased estrogen levels) get the best of me. As always, you have my promise that I will continue each and every day to strive to become a better father, man, and role model.

What I wanted to convey to you on that afternoon was not a criticism of your character, nor was it a challenge to your ability to manage your time. At no point was it my intent to challenge your emerging stature as a man or cause the biological repercussions associated with any challenges to your growing manhood. Those challenges and subsequent behavioral changes are much akin to the metamorphosis Dr. Bruce Banner experiences just before he turns into The Incredible Hulk (Lee and Kirby 1962). Oft times before you even recognize what is occurring to you, your burgeoning testosterone condition takes over your entire being and you become someone with whom I am unwilling and unable to have a meaningful conversation.

If not for the cruel trick that biology plays on you and me, we might have been able to have a conversation that was based more on substance and less on science. Unfortunately, without warning and certainly without intentions, we found ourselves engaged in a discourse that was going downhill fast. Now that a few days have passed and cooler heads have prevailed, I want to explain to you what I was attempting to convey…the Immutable Law of Reciprocity.
Son, sometimes HAPPY BIRTHDAY (caps purposely applied) is not just happy birthday (lower case purposely applied). Sometimes HAPPY BIRTHDAY is symbolic of so much more.

You will soon find out – and hopefully you learn this much sooner than later – that life, a good life, a quality life, and a successful life is one that has worthwhile relationships that have reciprocity as their essential foundation. Reciprocity, a give and take, a mutual appreciation, a shared value for one another is the key to real, authentic, longstanding relationships. Your relationship with each and every living thing on this planet is built on reciprocity.

Reciprocity begins with your relationship with God. God provides commandments for you to follow. When you follow those commandments, He finds favor in you and your life is blessed and He is pleased. When you choose friends, those relationships which will last beyond a semester or through high school will have as their foundation reciprocity. When you choose a wife, if that relationship is to survive where the majority of others fail, it will have to be built on reciprocity. Reciprocity simply cannot be avoided or ignored if you are to experience the type of relationships that you desire and enjoy.

So when I asked had you contacted your auntie to tell her HAPPY BIRTHDAY, I did so only to remind you of the Immutable Law of Reciprocity. Your auntie is a big advocate for major celebrations on birthdays. Since your very 1st birthday, she has always wanted to make it a big production so that you knew she considered you to be the most special nephew on the planet. From buying you trains that would not fit in our first family home (apartment), to taking you on trips all over the country and abroad, your auntie modeled for you her value of birthdays. You need only look to how she treats your birthday to know how she would like for you and others to consider her on her birthday – her one day to feel and be treated special – a day that she considers to be hers and hers alone.

What did you do on that day; you called her on the 19th hour of her special day? With only five hours remaining in her day, you called to say happy birthday. In the day of superior technology you could not come up with anything more innovative than a phone call in hour 19 of 24? Surely, a budding man of your advanced intelligence and social sagacity could derive an idea that would make your auntie know that not only did you understand the Immutable Law of Reciprocity but that you fully appreciate, respect and abide by it.

Trust me you will understand this more as time passes by.

Dad

<u>Questions</u>

1. What is the "law of reciprocity"? Why is it important to any relationship?

2. In this chapter, the father apologizes to his son. Why?

3. What is your routine for celebrating the birthdays of family and friends?

4. Do you have any ideas about what the son could have done to celebrate his auntie?

Chapter Thirty-Two: The Word is Trailblazer Not Trail-follower

Dear Naeem:

Several years ago, there was a commercial that quoted the saying "Lead, Follow, or Get Left Behind". I thought it was a catchy slogan, but I never gave much thought to what it meant. Lead, follow, or get left behind sounded simple enough, but what I did not know until much later was that this was a quote that describes the station in life that each person chooses to occupy.

What the quote meant was that we all have a choice. We can lead, we can follow those who lead, or we can be left behind. In your short span of time on this earth, you have been able to witness those who have led, those who have followed and those who have been left behind.

Sony once led in portable audio with the Sony Walkman. Today, Sony can only hope to follow Apple. Polaroid once led in photography. Today, more people use their iPhone to record video and pictures than ever before. When I was a kid (I know a long-long time ago on a planet far-far away) I wore Converse "Dr. J" sneakers. Today, Nike is the leader in the athletic shoes and apparel industry.

I know you are probably asking why any of this is important. The answer is simple. The aforementioned are examples of innovators and leaders...trailblazers if you will. Trailblazers – people who have decided that the path that the masses walk is no longer the right path to take. Trailblazers – people who have a dream and/or goal that cannot be fulfilled by following the same path that others who have failed continue to take. Trailblazers – people who understand the age old adage *"if you keep doing what you are doing you are going to keep getting what you are getting"* (Amos n.d.). Trailblazers – people who realize that humanity is built on, no humanity requires, people to innovate and evolve. A Trailblazer is you – Naeem Khari Turner-Bandele.

Yes, my son, you are a trailblazer. Of course, you don't realize it at the moment. I imagine most trailblazers feel as you do, a bit strange. Whenever we do something that we have never done before, we feel a bit strange. Doing something that we have never seen anyone who we know do makes it feel even more awkward. However, don't let the strangeness or the awkwardness of this situation make you think for one moment that you should be doing something else or something different. Remember, humanity is counting on you to blaze a trail where no trail previously existed.

As you prepare to take your sabbatical from the traditional US educational process, remain convinced that this is the right thing to do, this is the trail to blaze. Block out the comments of the Sony Walkman, Polaroid cameras, and Converse Dr. J's who try to get you to do what they are all doing (which in most cases is living a depressing, dissatisfying, discontent existence). Remember who these companies really are in both a literal and figurative sense – has-beens, those left behind because they failed to innovate, evolve, progress and change. Remember that those who want you to do other than blaze a trail are those who have always followed the trails that others have paved. Remember that those who don't want you to do anything other than what they are doing do so out of their own fears of change and progress.

Over the coming weeks and days, you will have many question the soundness of your journey to Brazil to train and play soccer exclusive of any academics whatsoever – in the greatest country for producing professional soccer players. You will hear many express concern over you finishing high school in the traditional four years, and then not going to college immediately upon receiving your high school diploma. You will hear many express their concern that you will miss out on getting your college degree and getting a job. You will hear many express concern because you will not declare a major before your eighteenth birthday, commit yourself to a profession that you are supposed to want to do for the rest of your life, and amass a great deal of educational debt in the process so that you will have to work in that profession for the greater part of your life to pay off the debt you incur.

Ignore this nonsense – block out all this ridiculous meaningless noise. Your nearly 4.0 GPA will be waiting on you when you return. Your membership in organizations such as the National Honor Society will be waiting on you when you return. Your AP credit and Honors class credit will be waiting on you when you return. The colleges and universities that thought you an excellent student will still think you an excellent student, if not more so, when you return (as you will have many life experiences that most of your peers will not have). Those people who are afraid of change will be waiting on you to welcome you home, and they will be doing the same things they were doing when you return. Hopefully you can see, there is nothing here that you will miss if you leave but there is a hell of a lot that you will miss if you stay.

If you stay, you will sentence yourself to a lifetime of "what ifs". What if I had gone? What if I had gotten better? What if I had the right coach? What if I was in the right environment? What if? What if? What if? What if? If you stay, you will sentence yourself to follow the same dusty path that leads to anywhere but where your dreams lead you. In the words of the sage Sarah Palin, you will sentence yourself to a "Bridge to Nowhere" (Henig 2008). If you stay, you will be sentencing yourself to be like all those who simply follow because they have always done so. But worse, if you stay you might more than likely be like the masses who have been left behind and don't even know that they are both behind and lost.

You know the U.S. system of developing soccer players is broken. You know the greater majority of US soccer players never get a shot to play in the best leagues throughout the world, i.e. Premiership, LaLiga, Serie A, etc. If you needed proof that the system is broken, you only need to look at the US's inability to qualify for the Olympics (Weir 2012). You know the U.S. system lacks creativity and innovation. You know that the system is built on race and socio-economic factors, more than it is built on athletic ability and individual commitment. You know that each year millions of American children register to play soccer in leagues that are incapable of helping them to get better or simply learn to play the "beautiful game" correctly. You know that each year millions of American children quit sports because of incompetent and uncivilized coaching (Kendrick n.d.). You know that each year millions of American children simply stop dreaming about being a great soccer player long before they have even had a chance to learn the process of making dreams a reality.

Naeem, go to Brazil! Go to Brazil and train until you can't train anymore. Go to Brazil and study the game until you are exhausted. Go to Brazil and compete until those whom you play against respect you like no American soccer player has ever been respected. Go to Brazil and leave no stone unturned. Go to Brazil and answer all the "What ifs".

When you return (if you return), you'll most likely find this country's educational and youth soccer systems to be just as you left them – followers and left behind. You'll find that your time away will have educated you far more than another year in high school. You'll find that your proficiency in your fourth language will have occurred much sooner and with greater ease than any of the other languages. You'll find yourself having grown as a man, as a conscious human being far more so than had you continued being with the masses of trail-followers. You'll find that your experiences will have others recognizing you as a pioneer of change. You'll find that as you tell your story others will agree that there is a better way and some, the smart ones, will begin to follow your trail.

Trailblazing, my son, is not something that you can do, it is something that you were born to do, something that you must do. In truth, trailblazing is synonymous with your name. I'm excited for you Benevolent King. I know it's been a long time coming but your time is now here.

Should you ever have any doubts while you are away that this is your time to experience change, remember to listen to a song written by the late, great Sam Cooke. The song is titled "A Change Is Gonna Come" and it's from Sam Cooke's 1964 album *Ain't That Good News*. The words that you should pay particular attention to are as follows:

> *There been times that I thought I couldn't last for long*
> *But now I think I'm able to carry on*
> *It's been a long, a long time coming*
> *But I know a change gonna come, oh yes it will.*

The time for a change is now. Blaze the trail my son, blaze the trail!

Love you,

Dad

Questions

1. Are you a trailblazer or a trail-follower?

2. What can you do to become a trailblazer at home, school, or in your community?

3. Why does the father warn against living a life of "what ifs"?

4. Is there noise in your life that keeps you from doing things you dream of doing?

5. Name some of the benefits the father believes the son will experience living abroad?

6. Do you know anyone who has ever skipped a year of high school to study abroad, travel abroad or follow a different path?

Chapter Thirty-Three: You Are Ready!

Dear Naeem:

I have little doubt that over the next several weeks, I will have to repeat these words to you over and over again: "YOU ARE READY!" You are ready - three simple words that are powerfully packed with great meaning. YOU – the most important single thing that I have ever done in my entire life. YOU – the single most meaningful relationship that I have ever been in or will ever be a party to. YOU – the absolute manifestation and proof that I existed on this earth and did at least one thing right. YOU ARE READY!

ARE is the verb which originates from the word "be". If I wanted to speak to you in my native tongue of Ebonics I would have written "YOU BE READY!" However, as this is not a lesson in Ebonics, I will skip my usual silliness for the moment. As this is no attempt at comedy, it is also neither an effort to give you a lesson on the present indicative plural nor second person singular of the word "be".

Rather, this is meant to remind you that the word "are" is an action word that signifies your current state of being. I did not say that "you were ready" meaning that the time had come and passed, and that you were no longer prepared. Nor did I say that "you might be ready", indicating that there was some possibility that you were ready, and there was also some possibility that you were not. Finally, I did not say that "you will be ready", suggesting that in time you will be prepared. Instead, my words were very clear and specific: "YOU ARE READY!"

So, it is time, my young warrior king, for you to do like the baby birds do each and every day. It is time for you to take your leave. It is time for you to leave the nest and fly.

I know there are moments when you worry that you are not ready. You will simply have to trust me when I say "YOU ARE READY" or in the words of Uncle Victor, *trust me when I tell you, boss,* YOU ARE READY. Even though I seem assured, you are probably still thinking "well dad, why are you so sure?" Well, I know you are ready the same way that a parent bird knows that their baby birds are ready to leave the nest. I know because I know. I know because intuition, instincts, nature and the universe tell me so.

When baby birds are born their parents must feed them every 15 to 20 minutes from about sunrise to 10 pm (Help...I Found A Baby Bird n.d.). This process occurs so that the parent can help the baby bird develop as soon as possible. The parents follow this exact process instinctually because they know it to be the correct course of action for their children. The baby birds are born without feathers so the feeding process not only helps them grow in size and strength but the process helps to develop the protective layer known as feathers.

Think about this process for a moment. Think about the love that parents must have for their babies to feed them every 15 to 20 minutes from sunrise to 10 pm. During a summer day, this feeding process could extend for 17 hours. For seventeen hours, each and every day, for about 3 weeks, parents search for food, fight off predators, deny themselves of nearly everything, endure constant states of physical, mental and emotional exhaustion and lack a general peace of mind. They do this solely so that they can protect and feed their babies every 15 to 20 minutes.

In a 3 week period, the parents feed their babies as many as four times an hour, 68 times a day or a remarkable 1,428 total times over a 3 week period. In the short span of three weeks, the parents provide their baby birds with more meals than the average person who eats three meals a day consumes over a period of a year. And to think, I thought I was a great father. These birds know how to make even me feel inadequate as a parent.

The parents take only three weeks to get their babies prepared to leave the nest. They do this not only for self-preservation, as they are exhausted and could not sustain the 15 – 20 minute feedings for 17 hours for much longer than 3 weeks, but they do it because it is a requirement for the survival of the entire family, not just the baby bird. Birds that are unable to leave a nest are easy prey for predators. Families that have to stay near a nest are equally subject to predatory risks.

Thus, birds want and need to be on the move so that they can avoid predators. Birds want their children to be able to fly as soon as possible so that the family can spread out (not being easy prey from being in and around the nest). Parents need their babies to be able to fly as soon as possible so that they can lead them to different spots every night, enhancing each one's chances of survival.

With that, the babies are kicked out of the nest and are expected to fledge (practice flying) for a short period of time until they learn to fly, can find their own food, and sustain themselves. Within a span of a few short weeks, baby birds are born and then expected to be fully functioning responsible birds.

Like the baby bird, you have been in a nest. However, you have had the fortune of being in your nest for much longer than a few weeks. For almost 17 years, your mom and I have done our best to make sure that you were kept safe and properly nourished (mentally, physically, emotionally and spiritually). For your entire life, we have done all in our power to protect you from the harsh elements of life and from those who sought to do you harm. We have watched you grow from a little bird with no feathers to one who is ready to strut and show off his grown and Peacock beautiful feathers. For nearly 17 years, we have watched as your wings have grown from nonexistent and fragile to fully formed and powerful like the Eagle.

So when I tell you that I know YOU ARE READY because I know; I mean just that. I know because I know. Like the birds, you will experience some moments of fledgling, but be mindful that this is only a small part of the process, and is not an indication that you are not ready. When those moments of fledging occur simply sit quietly and wait as nature, instinct, intuition and the universe step in to get you right on course.

Naeem Khari, He Who Is A Benevolent King, YOU ARE READY! YOU ARE READY to spread your wings and fly higher, faster and longer than anyone has ever flown.

It's okay! You can now leave the nest.

Dad

Questions

1. Why does the father believe that the son is ready "to leave the nest?"

2. If you have not already done so, you will eventually have to live on your own as a responsible adult. What steps can you take now to make sure that you're prepared like Naeem?

3. Can you imagine caring for something or someone enough to feed it every 15 to 20 minutes for 17 hours each day?

4. Why does the father make a big deal out of the meaning of the word "BE"?

5. What important thing does the father say the son means to him?

6. Why does the father routinely remind the son of his full name?

Chapter Thirty-Four: You Did the Right Thing!

Dear Naeem:

I am so sorry to hear about the state of your important friendship. Trust me, I know it is tough when you suffer the loss of a friendship.

My fraternity has as its motto *"Friendship is essential to the soul"* (Omega Psi Phi Fraternity Inc. n.d.). Implicit in these words is that our souls, all human beings, require friendship. Friendship is an indispensable element of life. However, the precise measure of friendship is unbeknownst to most of humanity, particularly those of us who live our lives merely on the surface of reality.

Instead, we miss the authentic nature of friendship because we fail to look beyond the body's superficial layer (the skin) to the parts of us that really truly matter: our heart, mind and soul. One cannot exist; no, one cannot know what it means to LIVE without friendship. Friendship has a collective importance to the progress and survival of humanity. Without friendship, humanity would cease to exist.

John Donne believed as the founders of my fraternity in the fundamental need for friendship. Proof of this shared belief is found in his quote *"No man is an island, entire of itself; every man is a piece of the continent"* (Donne n.d.). Mr. Donne realized the importance of friendship, and that friendship is at the heart of every successful moment in history.

The quote provides further insight that each man (woman) has to work in conjunction with one another, if their own "island", not to mention the entire "continent" is to survive. I only wish everyone, including your friend, understood the depth and breadth of these two quotes. Friendship requires a deep and unmitigated commitment to something larger than you, the "Law of Friendship and the Survival of Humanity".

I wish those of us who call ourselves a friend would realize that the foundation of true friendship is a contract that binds individuals through collaboration and reciprocity. In the words of Elbert Hubbard, *"In order to have friends, you must first be one"* (Hubbard n.d.). I believe the world would be a much better place today if the word friend was not used in such a lackadaisical fashion. Fewer disagreements would occur amongst people, fewer wars would be fought, fewer relationships of all types would cease to exist if we really understood and embraced the true meaning and responsibility of the word, friend.

Regrettably, the willingness to embrace, and the conviction to understand what I regard as the "Law of Friendship and the Survival of Humanity" is one of the great failures of mankind: man and woman. However, as a man, I must openly acknowledge that this is a tragedy which has been caused not by the shortcomings of women but almost exclusively through the failure of men.

Friendships are mostly imaginary and brief because as men we are typically the main promoters for the demise of these unions of the soul. We champion the destruction of our most essential unions because we fail to acknowledge that the quintessential element required in friendship is the surrendering and vulnerability of the soul. In essence, friendships are affairs of the heart. Yes, the heart – the part of us which men, even the "best" of men, do all that is humanly possible not to feel or acknowledge.

It is no wonder then that your friendship has deteriorated. If your role models and elders have not learned the value of the heart and its irrefutable role in friendships, how can you or any other young man be prepared to be a friend and participate in this union of the soul.

As a young man, society prefers to make sure that you are ill equipped to deal with the heart. You are bombarded with examples of so called manly behavior: real men don't cry; showing emotion means you are "gay"; keep your problems to yourself; men should figure things out for themselves, showing emotion makes you a sissy, a punk, and other derogatory expressions. These so called examples of manly behavior rob you of friendship's most essential requirement: the opening and sharing of your heart, your soul – showing emotion.

Instead of opening and sharing the soul, most men instead put up a ridiculously counterproductive front, acting as if they have everything together and are never affected by anything. The phrase we often use to express this friendship hindering behavior is "never let them see you sweat".

The truth of the matter is that while there may not be any sweat dripping from our brows, as men, far too many of us are slowly dying from stress, depression, anxiety, insecurities and other adversities that could easily be alleviated if we did not bottle them up, doing that which is contradictory to being human, a man. The bottling of emotions not only makes life challenging, but moreover it causes men to distort what it really means to be a human. The bottling up of our heart and soul robs us of the ability to process thoughts and make decisions that are best, not only for ourselves, but for the collective good.

Four years ago, as you well know, I lost an exceptionally good friend to this very situation. I lost a great friend because he forgot that friendship was essential to the soul and that no man is an island entire of itself. On September 15, 2008, two months to the date after his fortieth birthday, my fraternity brother, my real friend, my three dog, died from an assumed suicide. His refusal to open and share his soul was counterproductive not only to him, but to all those who were left to carry on after his death.

Although he has been gone now for almost four years, the wound feels as fresh as it did when I first learned of his passing. I wonder if your recognition, empathy and appreciation for how much I loved him and continue to mourn his passing had an effect on your decision to notify your friend's parents of his texts suggesting that he might no longer want to be amongst the living.

These last several days, I have wondered if the deluge of tears that you see cascading out of my eyes and down my face each and every year since his passing were the catalyst for you feeling compelled to reach out to your friend's parents. Even today as I attempt to celebrate the day of my own birth, I realize that you know that deep down inside I despise this day and have so for the past three years because today, my birthday is also his birthday.

Perhaps the disdain that I have for July 15th left you with a conviction not to ever have the feelings about any day without your friend as I have about living today without my friend. Maybe, your desire was not to feel the mounting guilt that I feel with each happy birthday wish (card, gift, text, email, etc.) that I receive on this day; insurmountable guilt for being alive to celebrate not just my birthday but his and my birthday without him. If any or all of these things crossed your mind when you notified your friend's parents about his uncouth and suicidal texts, I wish that I could say that I am sorry for affecting your decision making process but I can't. I am not sorry. Instead, what I can and will say is that I am so very proud of you. Stated more accurately, I am immensely proud of you.

John 15:13 says "Greater love has no one than this, that he lay down his life for his friends" (John 15:13 King James Version). While you have not done something as dramatic as giving your life for your friend, I want you to know that even if your friend, his parents or those closest to him never tell you, I want you to know that you unequivocally made the human, intelligent and responsible decision when you notified his parents. In the words, of Spike Lee, you did the right thing (Do the Right Thing 1989).

Your love for your friend is evident when you did that which now causes you pain. You laid down the chance to continue to be friends with someone under their misguided definition of friendship in order that your friend's parent might get him some help and so that he might live another day.

My beloved son and best friend, even if your "friend" never speaks to you again one thing is for sure – he is alive today. I would give almost anything to trade places with you – to have a chance to notify someone that my friend who was alive might be in trouble. I would give just about anything for my friend to be alive today, even if it meant that he would not speak to me. I can assure you that what I would give up to have him here on this earth would not be diminished or changed one bit based on whether or not he chose to speak to me after I contacted someone about the expression of his purported suicidal thoughts. All that would matter to me was that someone could hopefully check on him, and if needed, get him some help.

I can tell you this is how I would feel and approach the situation with absolute certainty. I can tell you this because I know what it feels like to lose a friend, a brother that you love. I can share with you the mental anguish of being continuously haunted by the thought that I should have known of my friend's mental state, and that I should have done something to help him, something that would have kept him alive.

I know the agony of dressing in a black suit, looking into a casket, driving in a long funeral procession, watching the casket being lowered into the ground, and knowing that you will never ever see that person again. I can tell you this because I know the pain you feel each time you reflect on the loss of someone with so much hope, promise and potential. I can tell you this because I know the shear hopelessness you feel when you look into the eyes of your friend's parents who are forced to do the unenviable, seemingly unnatural thing – bury their child and find the strength to continue living without him. I can tell you this because I have hated so many of my fraternity brothers whom I believe forgot the mandate that to have a friend one must first be a friend. Instead of nurturing our friend's soul, many of my fraternity brothers spent their time with him drinking, smoking, laughing, and partying, all the while those very things were inducing him to fall further and further into a pit of despair that he could not and would not ever climb out of. I can tell you this because at times I have hated myself for not being able to give him whatever he needed to make a different, better decision on September 15, 2008.

Son, you must know that you did the right thing! Don't ever, not even for one split second, think otherwise. One day hopefully when your friend matures and understands the true value and meaning of the word friend, he will see the correctness and the absolute necessity of your actions. One day, just maybe, even his parents who are fortunate enough to still spend time with their son, will thank you for alerting them of his state of mind.

Nonetheless, even if you and your friend never share a moment as friends again and/or his parents never acknowledge the love you had for their son, I know you did the right thing. My friend's parents know and would tell you that you did the right thing. My friend's siblings, family and friends who mourned his death as I did on September 15, 2008, and continue to mourn the shortness of his life each and every 15th day of July all know that you did the right thing.

On behalf of your friend and as a friend who lost a friend, thanks for doing the right thing! As a parent, who loves his son in the most indescribable manner and most incalculable measure, thanks for doing the right thing. Thanks for doing what I wish 30, 40, and 50 year old men, who espouse the words 'friendship is essential to the soul" as their life's motto, would have done. Thanks for having the courage, the respect for life, the understanding about the interconnectedness of humanity and the love for a friend, a brother, to do the right thing! I have been proud of you for so many things at so many times in your life, but I have never been more proud of you than I am right now.

With great pride and appreciation!

Your friend,

Dad

Questions

1. Why is the father proud of his son?

2. If you had a friend that was threatening to harm himself or herself, what would you do?

3. What responsibility do you have to your friends?

4. The father references "friendship is essential to the soul", what does this expression mean?

5. What things would you suggest the father do to deal with his grief?

6. Is there a particular day of the year that elicits bad memories? Can you imagine what it would feel like if that day was your birthday?

Conclusion: This Is Not the End

You may have reached the final chapter which says conclusion but in no way is this the end. I have learned as the father of the most amazing young man that there is no end to great parenting. Not only have I learned a great deal about parenting but I have learned even more about being a man.

Prior to writing Naeem, I'm unsure that I truly understood the meaning of being a man, the obligation of a father and my duty to the greater common good. Writing him has helped me considerably. There were times when writing him caused me to confront my own selfishness, fears and insecurities.

In the early years when I began to write him, I doubted his capability to grasp the importance of my words almost as much as I doubted my own ability to improve as a human being. I feared like most parents that the words (written words) I spoke would fall on deaf ears. Remarkably, writing him had the opposite effect. The more I wrote the better I understood and accepted my charge as a father. The more I wrote and the more he read, the increased understanding Naeem seemed to have about my mission as a father. The more I wrote and the more he read, the greater trust he placed in me – to aid him as he embarked on a concise and purposeful ascent to becoming a man.

My relationship with my son and writing him has made it easy to reflect on the things that truly matter and has encouraged me to remember that with each new day I have the opportunity and share with all humanity the responsibility to live life to its fullest. Thanks to Naeem, I now subscribe to the belief that as long as we are breathing and the sun rises, we have a new beginning – another chance to be better today than we were yesterday.

As I look back, I realized that watching him grow was a measuring rod of the usefulness of my words. The critique of his actions and accomplishments evidenced that not only did he hear me but he took heed to the things I said. He formed an incredible understanding of right and wrong. He developed a work ethic that is second to none. He cares deeply and passionately about all of humanity. He has exceeded anyone that I could have ever been and anyone I could have hoped to parent. I could not be more proud of who he has become and the upward trajectory of his life. I helped raise Naeem but Supaman has learned to fly on his own.

I now would like to encourage you to give your children a boost to help them reach incredible heights. My encouragement is simple. Write your children. Write them every chance that you have – daily, weekly, or monthly. The time frame you use to write is insignificant. What is important is that you write them to leave a written history of how much you love them, to share your hopes and dreams for them and to provide a roadmap for how to live a useful and purposeful life.

So bust out your pens and pads, turn on your tablets or open your laptops and get started writing. The world needs as many parents as possible to raise their own Supaman or Wonda Woman.

About The Author

Nathaniel A. Turner is a father, entrepreneur, motivational speaker and writer. He shares best parenting practices as a way of not only raising super children but as a way to change the world. He earned degrees from Butler University (B.S.) and Valparaiso University (J.D. & M.A.L.S). He resides in Indianapolis, Indiana. You can visit his website, The Raising Supaman Project, at www.raisingsupaman.com.

References

"1983 NCAA Basketball Championship." [March 26, 2008]. Video clip. Accessed March 26, 2008. YouTube. *www.Youtube.com*, http://youtu.be/8l5N2eKdvL4.

1989. *Do the Right Thing.* Directed by Spike Lee. Performed by Danny Aiello, Ossie Davis and Ruby Dee.

n.d. *American-Israeli Cooperative Enterprise.* http://www.jewishvirtuallibrary.org/jsource/Holocaust/olymp ics.html.

Amos, Wally "Famous" . n.d. http://superliminal.com/quotes.html.

Ankomah, Baffour . n.d. "Monkey Business Over Aids." *Virus Myth.* http://www.virusmyth.com/aids/news/namonkey.htm.

n.d. *BDEA/BuddhaNet.* http://www.buddhanet.net/e-learning/karma.htm.

Brothers, Joyce. n.d. http://www.brainyquote.com/quotes/quotes/j/joycebroth121 359.html.

"Cassius Clay vs. Sonny Liston." [February 17, 2008]. Video clip.
Accessed February 17, 2008. YouTube.
www.Youtube.com, http://youtu.be/LNdmySLkqyI.

Conrad, Steven. 2006. *The Pursuit of Happyness.* DVD. Directed by
Gabriele Muccino. Produced by Will Smith, Todd Black, Jason
Blumenthal, Steve Tisch and James Lassiter. Performed by Dan
Castellaneta, Kurt Fuller, James Karen, Will Smith, Thandie
Newton and Jaden Christopher Syre Smith. Columbia Pictures.
http://www.sonypictures.com/movies/thepursuitofhappyness
/.

Cooke, Sam. 1964. "A Change Is Gonna Come." *Ain't That Good News.*

Donne, John. n.d.
http://www.brainyquote.com/quotes/quotes/j/johndonne101
197.html.

Douglass, Frederick . 1845. *Narrative of the Life of Frederick Douglass, an
American Slave.* Mineola: Dover Publications, Inc.

2013. *Empire United Soccer Academy.* December 26.
http://www.empireusa-
syr.org/MemberResources/InTheNet/394748.html.

Franklin, Benjamin . n.d. *Brainy Quote.*
    http://www.brainyquote.com/quotes/quotes/b/benjaminfr15
    1603.html.

Franklin, Benjamin. n.d. *Brainy Quote.*
    http://www.brainyquote.com/quotes/quotes/b/benjaminfr12
    5394.html.

"Flutie's Miracle in Miami." [November 17, 2006]. Video clip. Accessed
    November 17, 2006. YouTube. *www.Youtube.com,*
    http://youtu.be/q3ykWbu2Gl0.

—. n.d. *Think Exist.*
    http://thinkexist.com/quotation/i_have_met_the_enemy-
    and_it_is_the_eyes_of_other/154906.html.

Haley, Alex, and Malcolm X. 1965. *The Autobiography of Malcolm X.* New
    York: Grove Press.

Hart, Clyde. n.d. "400 Meter Training." *North America, Central America
    and Caribbean Track & Field Coaches Association.*
    http://www.nacactfca.org/Hart-eng.htm.

n.d. *Help...I Found A Baby Bird.*
    http://www.messingerwoods.org/babybirds.htm.

Henig, Jess. 2008. *Bridge to Nowhere.* September 22.
    http://www.factcheck.org/2008/09/bridge-to-nowhere/.

Hubbard, Elbert. n.d.
http://www.brainyquote.com/quotes/quotes/e/elberthubb37 7954.html.

Jackson, Jesse. 1988. "Keep Hope Alive." *American Rhetoric.* July 19. http://www.americanrhetoric.com/speeches/jessejackson1988 dnc.htm.

Jackson, O'Shea . 1992. "It was a Good Day." *The Predator.* Song.

"James Buster Douglas knocks out Mike Tyson." [March 17, 2009]. Video clip. Accessed March 17, 2009. YouTube. *www.Youtube.com*, http://youtu.be/rt8LZ8FjGN8.

"Jesse Owens 1936 Olympics Adolf Hitler." [Jan 30, 2008]. Video clip. Accessed Jan 30, 2008. YouTube. www.Youtube.com, http://youtu.be/XXIe5GbLSUs.

"Joe Louis & Max Schmeling Weigh In 1938/06/22." [September 12, 2006]. Video clip. Accessed September 12, 2006. YouTube. *www.Youtube.com*, http://youtu.be/7TY28c-1vyQ.

Kendrick, Carleton. n.d. "Why Most Kids Quit Sports." *Alabama Soccer Association.*http://www.alsoccer.org/assets/959/15/Why%20M ost%20Kids%20Quit%20Sports.pdf.

King, Stephen , and Frank Darabont. 1999. *The Green Mile.* Directed by
    Frank Darabont. Performed by Tom Hanks, Michael Clarke
    Duncan and David Morse.

Lapine, Tom. 2009. *Bleacher Report.* July 5.
    http://bleacherreport.com/articles/212557-race-or-ignorance-
    why-more-black-nfl-players-get-arrested.

Lee, Stan, and Jack Kirby. 1962. *The Incredible Hulk.* New York: Marvel
    Comics.

2013. *Merriam-Webster, Incorporated.* December 26. http://www.merriam-
    webster.com/dictionary/love?show=0&t=1388099210.

Moss, Aron. n.d. *Entering Adulthood - the Bar and Bat Mitzvah.*
    http://www.chabad.org/library/article_cdo/aid/259492/jewis
    h/Entering-Adulthood.htm.

"Newscast from 1991 Duke beats UNLV." [May 6, 2007]. Video clip.
    Accessed May 6, 2007. YouTube. *www.Youtube.com*,
    http://youtu.be/okNOOcPmnZM.

n.d. *Omega Psi Phi Fraternity Inc.*
    http://www.omegapsiphifraternity.org/.

"Roger Bannister Breaks The Four Minute Mile." [May 31, 2007].
Video clip. Accessed May 31, 2007. YouTube. *www.Youtube.com*,
http://youtu.be/uz3ZLpCmKCM.

Roosevelt, Franklin D. 1933. *Inaugural Address*. March 4. http://www.c-
spanvideo.org/program/005792-01.

Siegel, Jerry , and Joe Shuster. 1938. *Superman*. DC Comics.

Smith, Will. 1998. "Just the Two of Us." *Big Willie Style*.

Southey, Robert Southey. 1837. *The Story of the Three Bears*. England:
Longman, Rees, etc.

n.d. *The Slave Trade*. http://www.crf-usa.org/black-history-month/the-
slave-trade.

n.d. *United States Holocaust Memorial Museum*.
http://www.ushmm.org/information/exhibitions/online-
features/online-exhibitions/nazi-olympics-berlin-1936.

Unknown. n.d. *Excuses*. Omega Psi Phi Fraternity, Inc. Accessed April
24, 1988. http://www.omegapsiphifraternity.org/.

Weir, Tom. 2012. *U.S. men's soccer fails to qualify for London Olympics.*
        March 27.
        http://usatoday30.usatoday.com/sports/soccer/story/2012-
        03-26/us-mens-soccer-fails-to-qualify-for-
        olympics/53796438/1.

Winfrey, Oprah. n.d.
        http://www.brainyquote.com/quotes/quotes/o/oprahwinfr13
        2401.html.

Young, Whitney M. n.d. *Search Quotes.*
        http://www.searchquotes.com/quotation/It_is_better_to_be_
        prepared_for_an_opportunity_and_not_have_one_than_to_ha
        ve_an_opportunity_and_not_/7936/.

"Young Woman and the Sea by Glenn Stout (long version)." [June 11,
        2009]. Video clip. Accessed June 11, 2009. YouTube.
        www.Youtube.com, http://youtu.be/IvXNhVGhfYQ.

Acknowledgements

My first and most important debt of gratitude goes to LaTonya Turner, the mother of Supaman. Thank you for waking me in the middle of the night nearly eighteen years ago to inform me that "it" (home pregnancy test) was plus. Without you there is no Supaman to raise. It has always been my contention (and I remain so convicted today) that no one - and I do mean no one - could have served as a better mother than you have for Naeem, particularly in his most important, foundational and formative years.

He is healthy and alive today only because you were willing to love him unconditionally, and do things for him that I could not conceive of doing (i.e. sucking the mucus from his nose when he was ill as an infant). I still marvel at those moments. I don't know if he really understands how quickly he would have died if those types of matters were left up to me. (Smile)

My second debt of gratitude goes to Gladys Turner, my mother, Supaman's grandmother. Without you giving life to me, there could not be a Supaman for me to raise. Moreover, without the compassion and never ending devotion you have shown me throughout my life, I am certain that I would not have learned the importance of expressing the deepest love and undying commitment to Naeem as authentically and openly as I have. I thank you for being the person who taught me not only how to love, but who showed me the importance of loving another human being.

I am also grateful to Tommie Turner, my father. Although our relationship has been a distant one for Naeem's entire life, I have found myself more than a time or two remembering a phrase that you would on occasion offer as your response to your own questionable behavior. You would say *"take what I do that works for you and apply it to your life, what doesn't work throw it out"*. When I heard you say these words, I considered the words to be cowardly and the words of a man who was simply too stubborn to make the effort to become better. However, when I became a parent, I found some value in those words. I have resolved to never offer my son a similar position statement simply, because I lacked the courage or commitment to be a better role model. I have instead applied those words as a reminder that while you and I may be estranged, there are things that I can take from your parenting methodology that were good and that could be applied to raising Supaman. I thank you for those good things and the recommendation that I throw away the bad.

A big thank you to the Village Counsel: men like Frank McKinley, Sr. (rest in peace), Grant Turner, Sr. (rest in peace), Gerald Sloan, Joseph Smith, Sr., Judge James C. Kimbrough Jr. (rest in peace), Robert L. Ursery, Sr. (rest in peace), Robert Ursery, Jr., Stuart Green, and numerous other men who stepped in and stepped up to the plate to serve in a surrogate father capacity for me when my own father was neither there physically, mentally or emotionally. I am forever grateful to you. Hopefully the way that I have raised Naeem makes you proud, and you recognize those efforts as one form of proof of my everlasting and eternal gratitude.

To the men whose friendship is unwavering and invaluable, the men whom I will forever recognize as the Men of the Village: Dr. Willie Underwood III, Gary Harris, Sr., Terrell Dunbar (rest in peace), Scott Sloan, David Lewis, Victor A. James Sr., Dr. Rick Hunter, Bruce D. Stephens and others: thanks to each and every one of you for your loyalty, inspiration and dedication. Most of all, thanks for the patience you have shown as you have listened attentively and reflectively to everything from my joy and pain to the happiness and sorrows of raising Naeem.

Last but certainly not least, thank you to the women of The Village: Adrana Davis, Ana Sloan, Arrie Ursery (rest in peace), Brenda Smith, Charlene Turner, Janine Green, Kimberly Turner (Auntie Kim), Monique Bernoudy (Auntie Monique), Ruth Betheaa (rest in peace), Sheila Trigg (Ma Trigg), Thelma Cunningham (rest in peace) and many others. Thank each and every one of you for loving me and giving me the much needed opposite sex, feminine, better/stronger gender perspective. Thanks for loving Naeem as if he was your own son. The wonderful mark that knowing you has left on my heart and soul is now an equally wonderful and indelible mark that now resides in Naeem.

There are so many others who could and should be acknowledged, but I must remember that this book is called Raising Supaman, and not that of acknowledging the whole world. In truth, there could be no Supaman without ALL the wonderful people who are, were and shall be members of The Village. If I have forgotten anyone, please chalk it up to my head and certainly not my heart. Thanks to all of you again. I am forever grateful and appreciative of all that you are, all you have done and all that you continue to do.

Nate

A.K.A.

Supaman's Dad

THANKS FOR READING

RAISING SUPAMAN

FOLLOW NATE AND
SUPAMAN AT
WWW.RAISINGSUPAMAN.COM